Table of Con

Preface 16

A little history of steam cooking 17

How does cooking with steam work? 18

Does steam cooking only work with an expensive steamer? ...20

How does the tagine work? 21

Electric steamers 22

Electric steamers - which device is the right one? 23

What should you watch out for when buying? 24

7 advantages of steaming 27

Which dishes are suitable for the steamer? 29

What should you watch out for when preparing food in the steamer? 30

100 recipes for every taste and every occasion 31

Appetizers 31

   1. Tomatoes with sheep cheese 32

   2. Marinated zucchini vegetables 32

3. Asparagus salad with strawberries 33

4. Rosemary potatoes with an herb and cream dip................34

5. Turkey skewers...35

6. Creamy lentil spread..36

7. Indian lentil soup (dal) with carrots and zucchini 37

8. Chickpea puree 38

9. Potato cheese - a recipe from Austrian cuisine 39

10. Spelled Cheese Salad...40

11. Steam eggs with bacon 41

12. Bean and tomato salad..42

13. Pear filled with cheese..43

14. Vegetarian wonton - 44

15. Warm chard salad 45

fish and seafood 46

1. Salmon fillet on spinach leaves 46

2. Salmon trout with zucchini risotto 47

3. Arctic cod with tomato rice 48

4. Pepper salmon with parsley potatoes - a quick Sunday meal
....49

5. Pangasius fillet covered with broccoli..............................50

6. Salmon in Swiss chard..51

7. Salmon and cucumber ragout 52

8. Salmon on ribbon noodles 53

9. Tuna casserole 54

10. Prawns on rocket 55

11. Fish skewers in the bed of vegetables 56

12.Halibut with herb carrots - particularly low in calories....57

13. Vietnamese style steamed fish...............................58

14. Indian fish fillets wrapped in spices 59

15. Seafood skewer..60

16. Octopus Salad..61

17. Hot prawn curry...62

18. Sole rolls with spinach filling................................63

19. Mussels in white wine stock..................................63

20. Citrus and herb sea bass 65

Flesh..66

1. Tafelspitz - a kitchen classic for the Sunday table 66

2. Sliced turkey with mushroom sauce...................................68

3. Beef roulades with ribbon noodles - perfect for Sunday lunch 69

4. Beef schnitzel with roasted potatoes 70

5. Turkey roulade with spinach 71

6. Herb schnitzel...72

7. Chicken "Asia" - very exotic...73

8. Minute steaks with green vegetables - a quick lunch 73

9. Stuffed chicken rolls with herb salad 74

10. Far Eastern Chicken - with lots of spices for an exotic aroma 76

11. Steamed meat - easy preparation and a quick meal.........77

12. Chicken breast wrapped in chard 78

13. Beef fillet in an herb coating - Highlight for the festive table 79

14. Lamb shoulder with couscous - an oriental pleasure......79

15. Steamed veal fillet - a poem with chervil.......................81

16. Butter-tender beef stew..82

17. Pollo Rosso - a delicious main course that tastes like a holiday!..83

18. Paprika goulash - nutritious and filling, just right on cold days! 84

19. Bohemian beer meat 85

20. Chicken paprika 86

Side dishes and vegetarian dishes 87

1. Vegetable lasagna - vegetarian and tastes good anyway...87

2. Turkish pudding...88

3. Tomato Gnocchi 89

4. Spinach and sheep cheese lasagna......................................90

5. Napkin dumplings 91

6. Swiss potato dumplings...92

7. Potato noodles 93

8. Stewed cucumbers 94

9. Ham pasta - a simple, quick dinner 95

10. Saffron rice with broccoli 95

11. Russian manti 96

12. Rocket risotto..97

13. Romanesco with ham and cheese sauce - a quick and savory lunch...98

14. Risi Bisi - very popular with children 99

15. Rice dish - a simple dinner 100

16. Rice pancakes - a sweet dinner and therefore popular with children. 101

17. Ratatouille - a classic insert, and not just since the cartoon of the same name. 101

18. Pasta with spinach leaves 102

19. Paella 103

20. Pumpkin risotto 104

21. Pumpkin cream soup 105

22. Cabbage rolls 106

23. Kohlrabi ragout 108

24. Potato soup - enjoyable and tasty 108

25. Potato dumplings 109

26. Semolina dumplings 110

27. Stuffed zucchini 111

28. Spicy leek casserole - a light vegetarian dish 112

29. Bread dumplings 113

30. Carinthian lentil soup 113

Desserts and sweets 114

1. Plum dumplings 115

2. Warm chocolate cake with a liquid core 116

3. Quark soufflé 117

4. Cottage cheese dumplings 118

5. Chocolate soufflé with a caramel core 118

6. Rhubarb compote with lavender sugar 119

7. Custard 120

8. Nut noodles 121

9. Apricot dumplings - a specialty from the Wachau 122

10. Exotic rice pudding 123

11. Almond wedges 124

12. Pumpkin and apple jam 124

13. Yeast dumplings with Powidl 125

14. Steamed noodles - a southern German specialty. 127

15. Creme brulée 128

Overview of cooking times: 129

Steam cooking for beginners:

The large cookbook with 100 delicious recipes for beginners, professionals and lazy people

Author: Dylan Kelly

Table of Contents

Preface 16

A little history of steam cooking 17

How does cooking with steam work?......................18

Does steam cooking only work with an expensive steamer? ...20

How does the tagine work? 21

Electric steamers..22

Electric steamers - which device is the right one?....23

What should you watch out for when buying? 24

7 advantages of steaming..27

Which dishes are suitable for the steamer? 29

What should you watch out for when preparing food in the steamer? 30

100 recipes for every taste and every occasion 31

Appetizers..31

   1. Tomatoes with sheep cheese 32

   2. Marinated zucchini vegetables 32

3. Asparagus salad with strawberries 33

4. Rosemary potatoes with an herb and cream dip................34

5. Turkey skewers...35

6. Creamy lentil spread...36

7. Indian lentil soup (dal) with carrots and zucchini 37

8. Chickpea puree 38

9. Potato cheese - a recipe from Austrian cuisine 39

10. Spelled Cheese Salad..40

11. Steam eggs with bacon 41

12. Bean and tomato salad..42

13. Pear filled with cheese..43

14.Vegetarian wonton - 44

15. Warm chard salad 45

fish and seafood 46

1. Salmon fillet on spinach leaves 46

2. Salmon trout with zucchini risotto 47

3. Arctic cod with tomato rice 48

4. Pepper salmon with parsley potatoes - a quick Sunday meal
....49

10

5. Pangasius fillet covered with broccoli..............................50

6. Salmon in Swiss chard..51

7. Salmon and cucumber ragout 52

8. Salmon on ribbon noodles 53

9. Tuna casserole 54

10. Prawns on rocket 55

11. Fish skewers in the bed of vegetables 56

12.Halibut with herb carrots - particularly low in calories....57

13. Vietnamese style steamed fish....................................58

14. Indian fish fillets wrapped in spices 59

15. Seafood skewer..60

16. Octopus Salad..61

17. Hot prawn curry...62

18. Sole rolls with spinach filling....................................63

19. Mussels in white wine stock.......................................63

20. Citrus and herb sea bass 65

Flesh..66

1. Tafelspitz - a kitchen classic for the Sunday table 66

2. Sliced turkey with mushroom sauce 68

3. Beef roulades with ribbon noodles - perfect for Sunday lunch 69

4. Beef schnitzel with roasted potatoes 70

5. Turkey roulade with spinach 71

6. Herb schnitzel 72

7. Chicken "Asia" - very exotic 73

8. Minute steaks with green vegetables - a quick lunch 73

9. Stuffed chicken rolls with herb salad 74

10. Far Eastern Chicken - with lots of spices for an exotic aroma 76

11. Steamed meat - easy preparation and a quick meal.........77

12. Chicken breast wrapped in chard 78

13. Beef fillet in an herb coating - Highlight for the festive table 79

14. Lamb shoulder with couscous - an oriental pleasure......79

15. Steamed veal fillet - a poem with chervil 81

16. Butter-tender beef stew...82

17. Pollo Rosso - a delicious main course that tastes like a holiday! 83

18. Paprika goulash - nutritious and filling, just right on cold days! 84

19. Bohemian beer meat 85

20. Chicken paprika 86

Side dishes and vegetarian dishes 87

1. Vegetable lasagna - vegetarian and tastes good anyway...87

2. Turkish pudding 88

3. Tomato Gnocchi 89

4. Spinach and sheep cheese lasagna 90

5. Napkin dumplings 91

6. Swiss potato dumplings 92

7. Potato noodles 93

8. Stewed cucumbers 94

9. Ham pasta - a simple, quick dinner 95

10. Saffron rice with broccoli 95

11. Russian manti 96

12. Rocket risotto 97

13. Romanesco with ham and cheese sauce - a quick and savory lunch 98

14. Risi Bisi - very popular with children 99

15. Rice dish - a simple dinner 100

16. Rice pancakes - a sweet dinner and therefore popular with children. 101

17. Ratatouille - a classic insert, and not just since the cartoon of the same name. 101

18. Pasta with spinach leaves 102

19. Paella 103

20. Pumpkin risotto 104

21. Pumpkin cream soup 105

22. Cabbage rolls 106

23. Kohlrabi ragout 108

24. Potato soup - enjoyable and tasty 108

25. Potato dumplings 109

26. Semolina dumplings 110

27. Stuffed zucchini 111

28. Spicy leek casserole - a light vegetarian dish 112

29. Bread dumplings 113

30. Carinthian lentil soup 113

Desserts and sweets 114

1. Plum dumplings...115

2. Warm chocolate cake with a liquid core 116

3. Quark soufflé..117

4. Cottage cheese dumplings 118

5. Chocolate soufflé with a caramel core 118

6. Rhubarb compote with lavender sugar............119

7. Custard..120

8. Nut noodles..121

9. Apricot dumplings - a specialty from the Wachau..........122

10. Exotic rice pudding..123

11. Almond wedges 124

12. Pumpkin and apple jam 124

13. Yeast dumplings with Powidl............................125

14. Steamed noodles - a southern German specialty............127

15. Creme brulée 128

Overview of cooking times: 129

Preface

At lunchtime, a kebab to go or a sweet piece of cake, in the evening a ready-made pizza from the microwave - this is the typical menu for many professionals. The family doctor says it at every check-up and every January 1st, the resolution is made to eat healthy and balanced food in the future. In fact, a low-fat, nutrient-rich and vitamin-rich diet with freshly prepared dishes every day is not difficult - with the right technology. A steamer is of great help in the modern kitchen. Gently enveloped in warm steam, each meal cooks in its own juice. It retains its natural aromas, water- and fat-soluble vitamins are retained and fruit and vegetables end up crisp, firm and colorful on the plate - what an appetizing sight! The best thing about steaming, however, is that it works almost by itself and overcooked vegetables and burnt meat are a thing of the past. Cooking with steam is not just in, but the ideal method of preparation for lazy cooks, professionals, newcomers to the modern kitchen, complete beginners and old hands.

How to do it, what equipment and kitchen equipment is needed and what needs to be considered so that the menu is on the table on time for meal time, can be read here. As is well known, no one gets tired of tips and good advice, which is why there are 100 recipes in our cookbook, for beginners and those switching, beginners and professionals, professionals and retirees. Have fun cooking and good luck!

A little history of steam cooking

Steam cooking is not a modern invention, thousands of years ago our ancestors used hot steam to prepare food. This method was particularly popular and sophisticated in Asia. Vegetables, pasta, stuffed dumplings or meatballs were put into small, round bamboo baskets and stacked on top of each other in a pot or wok filled with water. In other parts of Asia, small baskets with the food to be cooked were hung over a kettle of boiling water.

The ancient Romans also knew about the benefits of steaming food. In many Roman cities there were small restaurants open to the street, in which simple dishes such as lentils, beans, chickpeas or peas were prepared on an open stove. The food was kept warm in clay pots over steam. Those who were hungry and wanted to eat their fill for little money could get a portion of beans, lentils or peas from these cookshops, just like we get a sausage in the snack bar today.

Our grandmothers did not have any modern steamers either; they put a bowl of water in the oven with the food. The roast or cake cooked faster and remained moist.

Proper kitchen appliances and your own cookware for steaming were only developed by industry in the 1920s, but remained a niche product in this country. Only the pressure cooker was able to prevail. Steam ovens were mainly used in the catering industry. In the meantime, word of the advantages of cooking in your own juice has also got around in the fitted kitchens of medium-sized households. The new cooking trend began its triumphant advance in the USA before it found its way across the pond. However, modern steamers cannot be compared with the good old pressure cooker. Because while the pressure cooker heats the water to 120 ° Celsius with an overpressure of around 2 bar and thus cooks the food faster and saves time, modern steam cooking has nothing to do with speed. Steam cooking is more of a slow food, but still ideal for working people and lazy people because it works (almost) on its own.

How does cooking with steam work?

A saucepan and plenty of water are needed for cooking. The water gets hot, the heat is transferred to the food and at some point the potatoes are soft and the broccoli cooked and are drained off. Unfortunately, many valuable vitamins and minerals are water-soluble and are washed out of the food when it is cooked. At the end of the cooking process, the valuable nutrients are poured into the sink with the cooking water.

Steam cooking, on the other hand, works quite differently. The food to be cooked is placed in a container, which in turn stands above another container filled with water. The water is heated and the rising steam flows through the openings in the steamer. It envelops the food and heats it gently and gently. The food does not cook faster than when cooking on the stove or frying in the pan, but since nothing floats in the water, no nutrients are washed out! This keeps vegetables, fruit, meat, pasta and rice rich in vitamins, juicy, crunchy and tasty. The colors are also retained, as no color pigments are washed out. Broccoli, beans and peas are incredibly green, carrots stay bright orange and peppers stay bright red.

The taste experience is completely new, because cooking in its own juice means that its own aromas are retained. After all, steaming is also the low-calorie preparation method, as hardly any fat is used. Feast with pleasure while still paying attention to your figure - a dream will come true, right?

Does steam cooking only work with an expensive steamer?

Well, modern appliances such as electric steamers, convection ovens or steam ovens make cooking easier, but preparation using steam also works with simple means. Boil a saucepan with water and a well-closing cooking container that is hung or placed on top of the waterpot - no more cooks need to cook with steam. Fine sieves, woven bamboo baskets or very thin-walled metal bowls are suitable as cooking containers. A well-closing lid is important so that the water vapor does not simply escape into the kitchen. The cookware should be heat-resistant, after all, water only evaporates at a hot 100 ° Celsius.

Adequate stainless steel steamer inserts are already available for around 20.00 euros. A complete set with steamer and insert requires a little deeper grip in the wallet, but from 70.00 euros there are already very usable steamer pots with two to three inserts in specialist shops.

Carbon steel or stainless steel are the best materials for cookware because they are easy to clean, heat resistant and dishwasher safe. A good option for beginners in steaming and ideal for lazy kitchen helpers!

Bamboo steamers are all the rage. Cooking like in China may seem too complicated to a complete beginner in the kitchen, but in fact it is no witchcraft. Such a bamboo basket also offers many advantages. Bamboo is a natural material, yet it is very robust, heat-resistant and easy to clean. In addition, bamboo gives the dishes a very typical aroma and the food can be served fresh from the wok in the bamboo basket.

Traditionally, it can also be steamed with a tagine. The clay cooking pot with the conical lid and the typical shape comes from North Africa. In Morocco, Tajine or Taschiin does not only mean the steamer, but also the dishes prepared in it.
The tagine is made from clay or heavily marbled clay and burned at a low temperature. It is relatively thick-walled and can therefore withstand sudden changes in temperature unscathed. At the same time, the heat is transferred evenly to the food. The conical lid stores the heat for a long time.

How does the tagine work?

Water is poured into a small depression in the lid. The dishes are layered in the large pot. When the food is heated, the water in the food evaporates, the steam in turn condenses on the colder lid and the condensed water runs down the inside of the cooking container, where it evaporates again. Through this cycle, the dishes cook gently and in their own juice and get their very typical aroma.

For modern kitchens, there are now tajines with smooth bases that also fit on ceramic hobs.

Typically, tagines are not glazed, which is why they take on the taste of the food prepared in them over time. If you don't want this, a glazed tagine is recommended, it is also easier to clean. With the right recipes, even beginners can quickly prepare tasty dishes.

Electric steamers

The ideal device for beginners, beginners and lazy cooks, however, is the electric steamer. Almost every meal can be prepared in a time-saving, vitamin-rich and healthy way in the steamer. But not only the simple preparation is convincing, good devices can also be preprogrammed and allow the preparation of entire menus at the same time in one cooking cycle! Here in the cookbook you will not only find recipes for the steamer, we also want to make it easier for you to choose the right appliance.

Electric steamers - which device is the right one?

Numerous well-known manufacturers now offer steamers with more or less many functions and in different sizes. These include inexpensive models for beginners from around € 40.00. There is still a lot of room to go up and built-in combi-dampers can cost several thousand euros. What justifies these price differences are the additional functions, the intuitive operation, and the size and functionality of good devices. More expensive devices offer many more different functions, and often even recipes are integrated in the operating menu. They also make it easy to prepare a wide variety of dishes at the same time. Even fish and sweets or meat and fruit can be steamed at the same time without the different flavors being transferred. However, it does not have to be the most expensive steamer to get started, even devices in the middle price range have achieved good marks in product tests. What a good steamer should have is

• a programmable start function
• several preparation levels
• a keep warm function
• Quick to clean, dishwasher-safe steam trays and
• an integrated descaling function.

What should you watch out for when buying?

Before buyers allow themselves to be carried away into rash spontaneous purchases, it should be clear what the kitchen helper should and should be able to do in their own kitchen.

Is the device used regularly or should it only be used to produce a specific dish from time to time?

Does the kitchen offer enough space for a free-standing device and can it be stowed away to save space when it is not needed? If not, a built-in device might be better!

How many people do you cook for on a regular basis, what capacity is required? In a single household or for a small family with one child, a small steamer with a capacity of around 4 liters and perhaps two steam levels is sufficient. It is essential that these two levels can be operated separately in terms of temperature, cooking time and the beginning and end of the cooking process, as this ensures easy preparation and makes menu planning a lot easier. If, on the other hand, hungry hordes regularly wait for a delicious meal, a larger device with a capacity of around 8 to 10 liters is required.

Good steamers, regardless of whether they are floor-standing or built-in appliances, can do everything: bake, steam, keep warm and warm up. The keep warm function is worth its weight in gold if all family members come home at different times but still want a warm meal. Keeping warm and warming up not only saves the microwave, dishes are also warmed more gently and with less energy consumption in the steam. Above all, nothing can burn and even mashed potatoes, semolina or rice can be warmed up undamaged.

A steamer should enable easy preparation and save time and make work easier for working people as well as for thoroughbred mums. Therefore, a manually adjustable start time and individually adjustable cooking times and temperatures are a must. You program the kitchen helper, fill it with the food to be cooked and the appliance cooks while mum does the cleaning next door, does office work or helps the children with their homework. The device announces when the meal is ready with a loud beeping or buzzing sound.

A large display with easy-to-read numerical values and simple, intuitive menu navigation make operation child's play. The selected cooking menu, the set cooking temperature and the remaining time should be visible at a glance.

The time saved by steaming should of course not be undone for cleaning the device. High quality devices are dishwasher safe. Not only the cooking containers, but also other parts of the device such as cooking inserts for sauces or fish, partitions, etc. can be put in the dishwasher. An integrated decalcifying function in the water tank also saves tedious and time-consuming cleaning work.

High-quality devices have higher purchase costs, but they also allow separate programming of each cooking chamber, have an external steam generator and self-contained cooking levels, which means that different dishes can be cooked at the same time without mixing the flavors.

A wide range of accessories, such as cooking inserts for sauces, special cooking containers for rice and pastries and separate programs for baked goods, meat dishes and fish, also simplify operation and expand the range of applications. A special feature of high-quality steamers is the integrated cookbook. The recipes are structured so that they can be worked through step by step during the cooking process. Integrated cookbooks are a nice luxury, because in this cookbook you will find 100 recipes for preparation in the steamer that make cooking just as easy.

Finally, there are so-called combi steamers, which have an additional sous vide program. Sounds good, but the food must be vacuum-sealed in a heat-resistant plastic bag. A vacuum sealer must be purchased for this.

Combination steamers work at lower temperatures because the food is not continuously exposed to the hot steam, but steam is only released in spurts. This also means that the cooking times are longer. The price for a combi steamer is significantly higher than that of a conventional oven, and you also need a permanent water connection or a water tank that has to be refilled before it can be used.

7 advantages of steaming

1. All dishes are prepared in a way that preserves vitamins, is healthy, and is low in fat and salt. Since there is no food directly in the water, water-soluble vitamins and minerals are not washed out. Fat is not needed or only in small amounts. Meals prepared with the steamer are significantly healthier and lower in calories.

2. Colors, aromas and flavor are retained. Suddenly there are bright orange carrots, dark green broccoli and squeaky yellow peppers on the plate. With so many appetizing bright colors, even the youngsters can grab a vegetable side dish. The hot steam not only preserves the natural aromas of the food, but also lets fine taste nuances come through. Salt, spices and fat as flavor carriers can be largely dispensed with. This is also good for the desired bikini figure.

3. Burned- **on** food is a thing of the past, because nothing can burn when cooking in steam. The food also cooks much more evenly than when frying in the pan and without any fat. So you can safely leave the food to yourself and even go out of the house. On the other hand, you wouldn't just leave a pot of rice or potatoes on the stove and go to the neighbor for a coffee.

4. Modern steamers can not only cook, but also defrost, boil down, extract juice, bake, warm up and keep warm. Many devices have an automatic keep-warm function. They do not switch off completely at the end of the cooking process, but keep a slightly lower temperature of around 50 ° so that the food does not cool down.

Lunch stays warm for up to an hour if everyone comes later. Pre-cooked dinner is warmed up at 90 to 95 ° in a few minutes without losing its taste or the food drying, burning or becoming mushy. This process is called regeneration in technical terms and the fresh taste experience is actually convincing. Even the bread rolls from the weekend, which usually taste dry and stale the next day, can be regenerated in the steamer and then taste as if they were fresh from the bakery.

Frozen food gently thaws at a mild temperature of 60 ° without discolouring, drying out or cooking.

Jams and compotes can be quickly boiled down and the preserving jars are quickly disinfected in the steamer before filling.

You can even make yogurt yourself in the steamer.

5. Cooking with a modern steamer saves time. Instead of standing at the stove forever, stirring pots and pans and adjusting the temperature, simply put all the prepared dishes in the cooking baskets, fill the cooker with water, set the time and temperature and let the device work.

6. Steam cooking saves energy as all dishes are prepared together. Instead of several hobs on the stove, oven and microwave, only a single device is in operation.

7. Everything that can be boiled, baked or fried can also be prepared in the steamer.

Which dishes are suitable for the steamer?

Actually, all dishes can be put in the steamer as long as they are heat-resistant and have a well-closing lid.
Ceramic dishes are usually a little thicker-walled, which is why the food does not heat up as quickly. If you use ceramic dishes as a cooking container, the cooking time must be extended by approx. 5 minutes. The advantage of ceramics, however, is its ability to store heat for a very long time, which is why the food can also be served in the bowl and only cools down slowly.
Stainless steel cooking containers heat up faster and are very easy to clean.

Containers made of plastic or silicone are usually rather thin-walled and let the heat reach the food very quickly, but also cool down again very quickly afterwards. On the other hand, no germs settle on the plastic surface as long as it is undamaged.

What should you watch out for when preparing food in the steamer?

Basically everything that can be boiled, steamed, fried, grilled or baked can be steamed.

The cooking temperature is almost always 100 ° Celsius.

However, there are also foods or dishes that appreciate cooler temperatures and would be overcooked at 100 °: Meat products and fish fillets contain a lot of protein that curdles at high temperatures. Schnitzel, ribs, boiled beef, goulash or fish fillets are therefore best cooked at 75 to a maximum of 85 ° Celsius. Wienerle, sausages or other sausage products like a maximum of 90 ° C, otherwise they will burst.

Even a soufflé cooks really delicious at 95 °, while chocolate melts at 65 ° and only gets its silky shine at this rather mild temperature. Yeast dough can be steamed to rise, but 40 ° C is enough for the yeast to raise the dough.

Crystallized honey becomes liquid again at 40 ° and can then be eaten with pleasure.

100 recipes for every taste and every occasion

So, now the long-awaited steamer is in the kitchen. But how do you cook with it now?
Turn the pages and the most important part of the cookbook, the recipes, will come soon. Start vegetarian with a light starter, cook a main course on the second floor and top it with the side dishes. Sweet things for dessert shouldn't be missing either, and for a better overview there is a cooking time table at the end.

Appetizers

Starters open up a classy dinner, are a nice greeting from the kitchen or shorten the wait for the main course when the stomach growls.

With these 15 starter ideas there is something for everyone and they are prepared in no time and almost on the side.

1. Tomatoes with sheep cheese

87 kcal

Ingredients for 4 servings:
- ∴ *4 ripe tomatoes*
- ∴ *100g sheep cheese (feta or* herder *cheese)*
- ∴ *2 cloves of garlic*
- ∴ *1* teaspoon *chopped basil*
- ∴ *salt, pepper*

Peel and mash the garlic, cut the tomatoes in half horizontally and season with salt, pepper, basil and garlic. Dice the sheep cheese and spread it on the tomatoes. Heat in the perforated cooking container at 80 ° for approx. 10 minutes.

Serve with herb baguette or garlic toast.

2. Marinated zucchini vegetables

21 kcal

Ingredients for 4 servings:
        ∴ *1 large zucchini*
        ∴ *paprika powder*
        Chili ∴ *powder*
        ∴ *salt, black pepper*

Peel the zucchini and cut into bite-sized pieces. Season to taste with salt, pepper, paprika and chili powder. Cook in a closed container at 60 ° for about 20 minutes. Serve with flatbread or baguette.

3. Asparagus salad with strawberries

177 kcal

Ingredients for 4 servings:
        ∴ *400g fresh green asparagus*
        ∴ *400g fresh white asparagus*
        ∴ *250g strawberries*
        ∴ *3 spring onions*
        ∴ *40g fresh ginger*
        ∴ 5 tbsp *olive oil*
        ∴ 5 tbsp *vinegar*
        ∴ 5 tbsp *sherry*
        ∴ *salt, pepper*

Peel the white asparagus and cut off the ends. Peel the green asparagus only in the lower third, cut off the ends. Cut the asparagus stalks into pieces approx. 5 cm long and cook in the perforated insert at 100 ° for a maximum of 15 minutes.

In the meantime, wash, clean and slice the strawberries. Wash and clean the spring onions and cut into rings. Arrange the asparagus, strawberries and spring onions on a plate. Peel and finely chop the ginger. Mix together olive oil, vinegar and sherry and pour over the ginger. Season the marinade with salt and pepper and pour over the salad. Let it flow well.

4. Rosemary potatoes with an herb and cream dip

112 kcal

Ingredients for 4 servings:
   ∴ *800g potatoes*
   ∴ *1* teaspoon *olive oil*
   ∴ *1* tbsp *chopped rosemary*
   ∴ *250g sour cream or sour cream*
   ∴ *1 clove of garlic*
   ∴ *1 bunch of fresh garden herbs*
   ∴ *paprika powder*
   ∴ *salt, pepper*

Wash the potatoes and cut into wedges without peeling them. Spread the potato wedges in a closed cooking tray that has been brushed with olive oil. Sprinkle with rosemary and a little salt and cook for 45 minutes at 100 °. In the meantime, wash and chop the garden herbs (parsley, chives, chervil, tarragon). Press the garlic and stir together with the chopped herbs with the sour cream or sour cream. Season to taste with salt, pepper and paprika powder. Arrange the potatoes on preheated plates and place a small bowl with herb dip on each plate.

5. Turkey skewers

116 kcal

Ingredients for 4 servings:
- ∴ *500g turkey breast*
- ∴ *3 peppers*
- ∴ 4 tbsp *sugar*
- ∴ 2 tbsp *butter*
- ∴ *250ml chicken soup*
- ∴ *1* teaspoon *tomato paste*
- ∴ *3* tbsp *balsamic vinegar*

Wash, pat dry and dice the meat. Wash the peppers and cut into pieces of the same size. Place the meat and paprika alternately on wooden skewers, place on the cooking plate of the steamer and cook at 85 ° for about 20 minutes. Caramelize sugar in a saucepan and stir in butter and chicken stock. Simmer for 3 minutes and stir in tomato paste and balsamic vinegar. Season to taste with salt. Serve the turkey skewers with the sauce and some white bread.

6. Creamy lentil spread

99 kcal

Ingredients for 10 servings:
∴ *250g lentils*
∴ *50g quark, lean level*
∴ *50g natural* yogurt
∴ *1 spring onion*
∴ *1 clove of garlic*
∴ *1* tbsp *honey*
∴ *salt, pepper*

Put the lentils in a closed cooking container and fill with water until they are covered. Steam the lentils for 20 minutes at 100 °. Let cool and puree with the hand blender. Mix the quark and yogurt into the lentil puree. Finely chop the spring onion and garlic, mix with the lentil puree. Season to taste with honey, salt and pepper. Tastes delicious with baguette or pumpernickel.

7. Indian lentil soup (dal) with carrots and zucchini

319 kcal

Ingredients for 4 servings:
- ∴ *300g yellow lentils*
- ∴ 4 tbsp clarified *butter*
- ∴ *1* teaspoon *turmeric*
- ∴ *250g carrots*
- ∴ *250g zucchini*
- ∴ *1 medium onion*
- ∴ *approx. 500ml vegetable stock*
- ∴ *2 bay leaves*
- ∴ *1* tsp *garam masala*
- ∴ *1* teaspoon *mustard seeds*
- ∴ *curry powder*
- ∴ *cumin* powder
- ∴ *paprika powder*
- ∴ *1 lime*

Wash the lentils well under cold running water. Peel the onion and cut into strips. Peel the zucchini, halve lengthways and cut into slices. Peel the carrots and cut into even slices. Melt clarified butter in a pan, add spices and fry gently until fragrant. Add zucchini and carrots, fry briefly. Put everything in a closed cooking container, add the lentils and pour the vegetable stock until everything is covered. Cook in the steamer at 100 ° for about 15-20 minutes.

When the cooking time is over, let it steep for about 5 minutes. Squeeze the lime and stir the juice into the soup. Serve garnished with coriander leaves. If you love it spicy, cut a chilli pepper into small rings and serve them over the lentil soup.

8. Chickpea puree

222 kcal

Ingredients for 10 servings:
   ∴ *250g chickpeas*
   ∴ *50g* low-fat quark
   ∴ *50g natural* yogurt
   ∴ *1 onion*
   ∴ *1 clove of garlic*
   ∴ *1 bunch of coriander*
   ∴ *Caraway seeds, ground*
   ∴ *salt, pepper*

Soak the chickpeas in cold water for 3-4 hours, preferably overnight. Drain and place in the closed cooking container of the steamer. Steam at 80 ° for approx. 90 minutes. Finely puree the steamed chickpeas, mix with yogurt and quark. Peel onion and garlic and chop finely. Wash the coriander, shake dry and chop finely. Mix everything into the chickpea puree. Season to taste with caraway seeds, salt and pepper.

Tastes delicious as a spread and is vegetarian.

9. Potato cheese - a recipe from Austrian cuisine

171 kcal

Ingredients for 4 servings:
> 600g ∴ *floury potatoes*
> ∴ *1 cup of creme fraiche*
> ∴ *3 tbsp capers*
> ∴ *10 pearl onions*
> ∴ *4 pickles*
> ∴ *1 bunch of chives*
> ∴ *1 teaspoon mustard*
> ∴ *salt, pepper*

Peel the potatoes, chop them roughly and steam at 100 ° for

about 20 minutes. Finely chop the pearl onions, capers, pickles and chives. Press or puree the hot potatoes through the potato press. Mix the hot mass with the creme fraiche and all other ingredients. Season well with mustard, salt and pepper. The potato cheese is purely vegetarian and tastes great on fresh bread.

10. Spelled Cheese Salad

397 kcal

Ingredients for 4 servings:
- ∴ *250g spelled*
- ∴ *600ml water*
- ∴ *120g Emmentaler*
- ∴ *500g tomatoes*
- ∴ *1 bell pepper*
- ∴ *1 cucumber*
- ∴ *3* tablespoons of *oil*
- ∴ *vinegar*
- ∴ *salt, pepper*

Put the spelled in a bowl, cover with water and let stand for a few hours. Then put the rest of the water in a closed container and steam at 100 ° for about 40 minutes. Wash tomatoes, peppers and cucumber and cut into bite-sized pieces. Dice the

Emmentaler and mix everything with the steamed spelled. Mix a marinade with oil, vinegar, salt and pepper and pour over the salad. Stir in, let it steep briefly and serve.

11. Steam eggs with bacon

226 kcal

Ingredients for 4 servings
∴ *4 eggs*
∴ *200g diced bacon*
∴ *1 onion*
∴ *60g celery*
∴ *1 clove of garlic*
∴ *2* tbsp *white balsamic vinegar*
∴ *1* tbsp *sugar*
∴ *100ml white wine*
∴ *300ml cream*

For the steamed eggs you need mason jars or jam jars with a large opening, which are brushed with a little oil. Beat the eggs and slide one egg into each glass. Close the jar and steam at 100 ° for a maximum of 4 minutes. Leave the bacon cubes in a pan without fat, set aside some. Add sugar and let it caramelize. Finely dice the onion, garlic and celery and roast in the pan. Deglaze with vinegar, add wine and cream and simmer for a few minutes. Puree everything and distribute on the steamed eggs, sprinkle with the remaining bacon cubes.

12. Bean and tomato salad

185 kcal

Ingredients for 4 servings:
∴ *500 g green beans*
∴ *4 sprigs of savory*
∴ *2* tbsp *lemon juice*
∴ *2* teaspoons of *mustard*
∴ *2* tbsp *olive oil*
∴ *3 tomatoes*
∴ *6 leaves of basil*
∴ *salt, pepper*

Wash the beans and break through in the middle. Put the savory in the closed container and steam at 100 ° for 30 minutes. For the salad marinade, mix the lemon juice, mustard, olive oil, salt and pepper together well. Wash and dice tomatoes. Add the steamed beans to the marinade and mix well. Add tomatoes and sprinkle with chopped basil leaves.

13. Pear filled with cheese

225 kcal

Ingredients for 4 servings:

∴ *4 pears (Abate Fetel, Kaiser Alexander or Alexander Lucas)*

∴ *2 lemons*

∴ *100g* blue *cheese*

∴ *6* tbsp heavy *cream*

∴ *2* tablespoons of *chopped parsley*

∴ *2* tbsp *chopped walnuts*

∴ *salt, pepper*

Squeeze the lemons. Wash, peel and halve the pears lengthways, remove the core. Rub pears with lemon juice so they don't turn brown. Cook softly in the steamer in a closed container at 100 ° for 20 minutes. The pears should still be firm to the bite! Mash the blue cheese and mix with the cream. Hollow out the pear halves with a teaspoon, mash the pulp and mix with the cheese. Season with salt and pepper and divide into the pear halves. Sprinkle with parsley and nuts. The pears taste vegetarian and very fruity as a snack or as a starter!

14. Vegetarian wonton -

slightly more elaborate starter from Asia. The ingredients are available in the Asia store or can also be ordered over the Internet.

119 kcal

Ingredients for 4 servings
  ∴ *3 spring onions*
  ∴ *2 cloves of garlic*
  ∴ *2 tbsp grated ginger*
  ∴ *2 tbsp chives*
  ∴ *400g white cabbage or savoy cabbage*
  ∴ *2 tbsp sweet chili sauce*
  ∴ *3 tbsp chopped coriander*
  ∴ *50g water chestnuts*
  ∴ *25 wonton sheets*
  ∴ *1 tbsp soy sauce*
  ∴ *1 tbsp lime juice*
  ∴ *1 red chilli pepper*
  ∴ *sesame oil*
  ∴ *peanut oil*

Cut the spring onion into small rings. Peel and finely dice the garlic. Peel the ginger and grate finely. Wash and finely chop the chives. Wash and finely chop the coriander. Chop water chestnuts. Heat the oil in a pan, fry the onion, ginger, garlic and chives in it for 2 minutes. Turn up the heat and add the cabbage leaves, fry for about 5 minutes. Mix in the chili sauce, coriander and water chestnuts and let everything cool down. Pour off excess water. Lay out the wonton leaves on a smooth surface and place a heaping teaspoon of filling on each leaf. Moisten the dough tips with water and close the pockets. Put the dumplings in a perforated container and steam at 100 ° for 5 minutes. For the dip, mix the sesame oil, peanut oil, soy sauce and lime juice with the chopped chilli. The wontons taste even better when you steam them in a bamboo basket. To do this, boil some water in a saucepan, line the bamboo basket with baking paper and fill with the dumplings. Hang the basket in the pot (do not put it directly in the water!), Cover and steam for 5 minutes.

15. Warm chard salad

166 kcal

Ingredients for 4 servings:
 ∴ *1 kg of* Swiss *chard*
 ∴ *4* tbsp *olive oil*
 ∴ *1 lemon*
 ∴ *salt, pepper*

Wash the chard, remove the stalks. Steam at 100 ° for 12 minutes until it collapses. Coarsely chop and place in a bowl. Squeeze the lemon and mix the juice, olive oil, salt and pepper into a marinade. Pour the dressing over the warm Swiss chard and serve with fresh flatbread and a few olives.

fish and seafood

Fish is not for everyone, but steamed, it can be cooked wonderfully tender and precisely to the point. Salmon, cod and tuna are classics and may convince many a fish grouch with delicious side dishes. The steamer is not only good for fish, which is why we naturally didn't want to withhold recipes with seafood from you.

1. Salmon fillet on spinach leaves

294 kcal

Ingredients for 4 servings:
    ∴ *4 salmon fillets*
    ∴ *1 onion*
    ∴ *1 clove of garlic*
    ∴ *200g spinach leaves, frozen goods*
    ∴ *1 lemon*

∴ *nutmeg*

∴ *salt, pepper*

Thaw and drain the spinach leaves. Peel, finely chop the onion and garlic and mix well. Place the salmon fillets on the cooking plate of the steamer and season with half of the onion and garlic mixture, salt, pepper and nutmeg. Cook the fillets at 100 ° for about 20 minutes.

Put the spinach leaves in a perforated cooking container, season with the rest of the onion-garlic mixture, salt and pepper. Cook the spinach for 8-10 minutes at 100 °.

Place the salmon with a slice of lemon on the spinach leaves on preheated plates. It goes well with steamed potatoes or rice.

2. Salmon trout with zucchini risotto

381 kcal

Ingredients for 4 servings:

∴ *2 salmon trout*

300g ∴ *risotto rice, alternatively short grain rice*

∴ *550ml vegetable stock*

∴ *200ml dry white wine*

∴ *2 zucchinis*

∴ *10 cocktail tomatoes*

∴ 1 tbsp *butter*

∴ *1 corner of cheese spread*

∴ *salt, pepper*

Put the rice with the vegetable stock, the wine, salt and pepper in a closed cooking bowl. Steam for 10 minutes at 100 °. Wash the zucchini and cut into small cubes, place in a perforated cooking tray. Brush another perforated cooking container with the butter and add the salmon trout. Cook the zucchini and salmon trout for 15 minutes at 85 °. Meanwhile, cut the cocktail tomatoes into small pieces. Finally fold the zucchini, tomatoes, butter and cheese spread into the risotto. Serve with the salmon.

3. Arctic cod with tomato rice

211 kcal

Ingredients for 4 servings:

∴ *8 pieces of* polar cod fillet

∴ *200g basmati rice*

∴ *1 can of chopped tomatoes*

∴ *150g sugar* snap *peas*

∴ 2 tbsp *Italian herbs*

∴ *100ml water*

Spice ∴ *mix for fish*

∴ *salt, pepper*

Put rice in a closed container or a special rice cooking container. Cut the sugar snap peas into bite-sized pieces and add to the rice. Add tomatoes and water. Season with salt, pepper and the Italian herbs. Mix well and cook for 20 minutes at 100 °. Season the fish fillets with the seasoning mix for fish. Steam in a closed container at 85 ° for 8 minutes.

Serve the polar cod on the tomato rice. The dish is especially popular with children.

4. Pepper salmon with parsley potatoes - a quick Sunday meal

461 kcal

Ingredients for 4 servings:
∴ *600g salmon*
∴ *8 potatoes*
∴ *1 bunch of parsley*
∴ *1* teaspoon *colored pepper, crushed*
∴ *8* tbsp *olive oil*
∴ *1* teaspoon *salt*

Wash the salmon and pat dry, rub with salt and crushed pepper, drizzle with 2 tablespoons of olive oil. Place in a closed cooking tray and cook for 10 minutes at 85 °. Pluck the parsley from the stems and chop.

Peel the potatoes, cut into cubes and cook in a closed cooking tray for 20 minutes at 100 °. Heat 2 tablespoons of olive oil in a pan, add the potatoes, season with salt, toss a little, remove from the fire. Add parsley and mix well. Arrange salmon and parsley potatoes on plates and serve immediately.

5. Pangasius fillet covered with broccoli

(Recipe for 4 people)
269 kcal

Ingredients for 4 servings:
        ∴ *400g broccoli*
        ∴ *3 egg yolks*
        ∴ *3* tbsp *flour*
        ∴ *1* pinch of *baking powder*
        ∴ *4 pangasius* fillets
        ∴ *salt, pepper*

Divide broccoli into small florets and steam in a perforated container for 6 minutes at 100 °. Coarsely puree the slightly cooled broccoli with a hand blender. Mix the broccoli puree with egg yolks, flour and baking powder and season with salt and pepper. Rub the fish fillets with salt and pepper and brush with the broccoli mixture. Cook the fish fillets in the perforated cooking tray for 10 minutes at 90 °.

Boiled potatoes or rice are suitable as a side dish.

6. Salmon in Swiss chard

128 kcal

Ingredients for 4 servings:
- ∴ *4 salmon fillets*
- ∴ *700g Swiss chard*
- ∴ 4 tbsp *lemon juice*
- ∴ 4 tbsp *tomato paste*
- ∴ *400ml water*
- ∴ *400g cherry tomatoes*
- ∴ 2 tbsp *olive oil*
- ∴ *1/2* teaspoon *sugar*
- ∴ *salt, pepper*

Wash the chard leaves and cut out the stalks. Cut the stems into strips. Blanch the leaves in salted water for 30 seconds, rinse with cold water and pat dry with kitchen paper. Drizzle the salmon fillets with lemon juice and season with salt.

Place 2 chard leaves on top of each other, place a fish fillet in the middle and wrap the leaves. Place the fish parcels in a steamer and cook for 10-15 minutes at 85 °. Halve the cherry tomatoes. Heat the oil and steam the chard stalks cut into strips for 3 minutes. Add tomatoes and cook for another 3 minutes, then season with salt, pepper and sugar. Add tomato paste and water and stir carefully, bring to the boil.

Place the salmon on a plate and serve with the chard and tomato sauce.

7. Salmon and cucumber ragout

289 kcal

Ingredients for 4 servings:
- *∴ 700g salmon*
- *∴ 1000g cucumber*
- *∴ 100ml vegetable stock*
- *∴ 3 teaspoons of mustard*
- *∴ 120g natural yogurt*
- *∴ lemon juice*
- *∴ 1/2 bunch of dill*
- *∴ salt, pepper*

Rinse the salmon with cold water, pat dry and cut into large cubes. Peel the cucumber and cut into small pieces. Put both in a closed cooking bowl and season with salt, pepper and lemon juice. Pour in the broth. Finely chop the dill and stir in. Let steam for 15 minutes at 85 °.

Mix the yogurt with mustard well and stir into the salmon and cucumber mixture before serving.

8. Salmon on ribbon noodles

644 kcal

Ingredients for 4 servings:
- ∴ *500g ribbon noodles*
- ∴ *200g mixed vegetables, frozen goods*
- ∴ *200g salmon fillet*
- ∴ *100ml cream*
- ∴ 5 tbsp *creme fraiche*
- ∴ 1 tbsp *chopped herbs*
- ∴ 1 teaspoon of *soup powder*
- ∴ *salt, pepper*

Cook the pasta in plenty of salted water until al dente and strain. Put mixed vegetables in a bowl and let thaw slightly. Cut the salmon into pieces. Put the pasta in a closed cooking bowl, spread the mixed vegetables and salmon on top. Mix the creme fraîche, cream, chopped herbs, salt, pepper and soup powder in a bowl and pour over the pasta. Lightly salt and pepper the salmon and spread over the pasta. Let everything cook for 10 minutes at 85 °.

9. Tuna casserole

288 kcal

Ingredients for 4 servings:
- ∴ *200g of pasta*
- ∴ *1 zucchini*
- ∴ *2 carrots*
- ∴ *2 cans of tuna with vegetable* sauce
- ∴ *2 cloves of garlic*
- ∴ *1/2 cup of cream*
- ∴ *4 tbsp parmesan*
- ∴ *salt, pepper*

Wash the zucchini and cut into coarse strips. Peel the carrot and cut into fine strips. Peel and finely chop the garlic and fry in hot oil. Add the carrots and zucchini and fry with them. Pour on the cream and simmer a little. Put the pasta in a closed cooking bowl and mix with the vegetable sauce and tuna. Season with salt and pepper. Cook the casserole at 100 ° for 20 minutes. Served sprinkled with parmesan.

10. Prawns on rocket

267 kcal

Ingredients for 4 servings:
- *∴ 16 prawns*
- *∴ 2 cloves of garlic*
- *∴ 16 capers*
- *∴ 300g rocket*
- *∴ 1/2 l fish* stock
- *∴ 1/4 l white wine*
- *∴ 2 tomatoes*
- ∴ 2 teaspoons of *white balsamic vinegar*
- ∴ 1 teaspoon *starch*
- ∴ 1 tbsp *lemon juice*
- ∴ 1 tbsp *olive oil*
- *∴ 6 leaves of fresh basil*
- *∴ salt, pepper*

Let the white wine, fish stock and balsamic vinegar reduce a little in a saucepan. Mix in the cornstarch in 3 tablespoons of cold water, season everything with salt and pepper and keep warm. Wash and peel the prawns and remove the intestines with a sharp knife. Place in a closed cooking bowl, season with salt, pepper and drizzle with lemon juice and olive oil. Steam the prawns for 3 minutes at 85 ° C.

Peel the garlic and cut into leaves, pluck the basil, dice the tomatoes. Sprinkle over the prawns together with the capers and continue steaming for 1-2 minutes.

Spread the washed rocket on the plates, place the prawns on top and pour the white wine sauce over them.

11. Fish skewers in the bed of vegetables

185 kcal

Ingredients for 4 servings:
  ∴ *650g monkfish*
  ∴ *3 zucchini*
  ∴ *1* Swiss *chard*
  ∴ *1 yellow* pepper
  ∴ *1 red* pepper
  ∴ *lemon juice*
  ∴ *Garlic* granules
  ∴ *6 sprigs of rosemary*
  ∴ *salt, pepper*

Cut the fish into cubes of the same size, drizzle with lemon juice and season with salt and pepper. Skewer the pieces of fish one by one on the rosemary sprigs.

Peel the zucchini and cut into small pieces. Wash and dice the peppers. Season the paprika and zucchini with garlic granules, salt and pepper. Divide the chard into individual leaves, shorten the stems and place in a closed container. Place the zucchini and paprika on the chard leaves, place the fish skewers on the bed of vegetables. Cook everything for 10 minutes at 85 °.

12.Halibut with herb carrots - particularly low in calories

73 kcal

Ingredients for 4 servings:
- ∴ *4 halibut chops*
- ∴ *500g carrots with greens*
- ∴ 4 tbsp *dill*
- ∴ 4 tbsp *parsley*
- ∴ *1* tbsp *salt*
- ∴ 2 teaspoons of *butter*
- ∴ *2 lemons*
- ∴ *pepper*

Peel and wash the carrots and leave about 2 cm of the green. Cook the whole carrots in a closed container at 100 ° for 20 minutes. Rinse the fish with cold water, pat dry and drizzle with lemon juice. Cook the fish chops for 20 minutes at 85 ° on the cooking plate. Add butter to the finished carrots. Chop the herbs and sprinkle over the carrots. Spread the carrots on plates and place the fish on top.

13. Vietnamese style steamed fish

242 kcal

Ingredients for 4 servings:
 ∴ *850g fish fillet (pangasius, salmon)*
 ∴ *1 onion*
 ∴ *5 chili peppers*
 ∴ *1 tbsp fish sauce*
 ∴ *1 piece of ginger*
 ∴ *1 stalk of lemongrass*
 ∴ *2 kaffyr lime leaves*
 ∴ *2 leaves of Thai basil*

Peel the ginger and grate finely. Cut the lemongrass into small pieces. Cut the chilli peppers into small pieces with a sharp knife. Peel and dice the onion. Wash the fish and pat dry. Wash the basil and lime leaves, shake dry and finely chop.

Puree the lemongrass, ginger, chilli and onion into a paste with the mixer. Brush the fish well with the paste. Sprinkle with lime leaves and basil. Steam in a closed container at 85 ° for 20 minutes. Rice goes well with it.

14. Indian fish fillets wrapped in spices

235 kcal

Ingredients for 4 servings
- *∴ 600g fish fillets*
- *∴ 1 chilli pepper*
- *∴ 1 onion*
- *∴ 3 cloves of garlic*
- *∴ 2 stalks of coriander*
- ∴ *1* teaspoon *coriander seeds*
- ∴ *1/2* teaspoon *turmeric*
- ∴ *1/2* teaspoon *pepper*
- ∴ *1* tbsp *fish sauce*
- ∴ *2* tbsp *coconut milk*
- ∴ *2* tbsp *rice flour*
- ∴ *1 egg*

Peel and dice the onion. Peel the garlic and chop it into small pieces. Wash, shake and finely chop the coriander leaves. Cut the chilli pepper into small pieces with a sharp knife. Wash the fish fillets, pat dry and cut into strips. Grind or puree the garlic, chilli, onion, coriander, and coriander seeds into a paste. Beat the egg in a bowl and mix with the turmeric, pepper, fish sauce and coconut milk. Turn the fish strips first in the sauce and then in rice flour. Steam the fish for 20 minutes at 85 °. Arrange on preheated plates and garnish with the chilli. Basmati rice goes well with it.

15. Seafood skewer

(Recipe for 4 people)
206 kcal

Ingredients for 4 servings:
∴ *500g fish fillet*
∴ *8* king *prawns*
∴ *3 peppers*
∴ *2* tbsp *thyme*
∴ *2* tbsp *lemon juice*
∴ *salt, pepper*

Wash the peppers, remove the core and cut into pieces of the same size.

Wash the fish fillets, pat dry and cut into small pieces. Peel the prawns and remove the intestines. Place the fish, prawns and peppers alternately on wooden skewers and drizzle with lemon juice. Finely chop the thyme. Sprinkle the skewers with thyme, season with salt and pepper. Steam the skewers on the cooking plate of the steamer for 12 minutes at 90 °. A fresh salad and white bread go well with it.

16. Octopus Salad

202 kcal

Ingredients for 4 servings:
- ∴ *3 octopuses*
- ∴ *3 large potatoes*
- ∴ *2 stalks of* celery
- ∴ 4 tbsp *olive oil*
- ∴ *1/2* tbsp *lemon juice*
- ∴ *salt, pepper*

It's best to have the fishmonger clean the octopus. Wash the octopus and cook for 40-50 minutes at 90 ° until soft. Peel the potatoes, cut into cubes and cook for 17 minutes at 100 °. Cut the celery stalks and fry them in a tablespoon of olive oil. Add the potato cubes and another tablespoon of olive oil and continue frying. Let the cooked octopus cool down a bit, cut into bite-sized pieces and mix with the potatoes and celery. Season to taste with salt, pepper, olive oil and lemon juice.

17. Hot prawn curry

(Recipe for 4 people)

355 kcal

Ingredients for 4 servings:
∴ *450g prawns*
∴ *1 zucchini*
∴ *450ml coconut milk*
∴ *1 dash of fish sauce*
∴ 5 tbsp *curry paste*
∴ *3 chili peppers*
∴ 1 tbsp *lemon juice*
∴ 1 tbsp *chopped chives*
∴ *salt, pepper*

Puree the curry paste and coconut milk, add salt, lemon juice and fish sauce.

Wash and clean the zucchini and cut into small pieces. Place the prawns and zucchini in a closed bowl. Finely chop the chilli peppers. Add the chilli and curry sauce to the prawns and cook for 5 minutes at 90 °. Serve sprinkled with chopped chives. Rice goes well with it.

18. Sole rolls with spinach filling

89 kcal

Ingredients for 4 servings:
  ∴ *4 fillets of sole*
  ∴ *120g spinach leaves*
  ∴ *1 bunch of chives*
  ∴ *lemon juice*
  ∴ *salt, pepper*

Wash sole fillets, pat dry and season with salt, pepper and a little lemon juice. Remove the ribs from the spinach and spread over the fillets. Roll up the fish fillets tightly and tie each one with a stalk of chives. Cook the fish rolls in the perforated cooking tray for 14 minutes at 85 °.

19. Mussels in white wine stock

416 kcal

Ingredients for 4 servings:

∴ *1000 - 1200g mussels*

∴ *2 onions*

∴ *4 cloves of garlic*

∴ *2 carrots*

∴ *1 celery* bulb

∴ *2 leeks*

∴ *400ml dry white wine*

∴ 6 tbsp *olive oil*

∴ 4 tbsp *chopped herbs*

∴ *salt, pepper*

Thoroughly brush the mussels under cold, running water to remove any sand and limescale residue. Peel off the beards with your fingers. Throw away any mussels that have already been opened. Pour the mussels into a sieve, rinse again thoroughly and allow to drain. Peel onion and garlic and chop finely. Clean and wash the carrots, celery and leek and cut into bite-sized pieces. Squeeze the lemon.

Heat olive oil in a pot. Sweat the onion and garlic until translucent, add the vegetables. Sweat everything for 4 to 5 minutes while stirring. Pour in white wine and lemon juice, sprinkle with herbs and season the stock with salt and pepper.

Spread the mussels in a closed cooking bowl and pour the white wine stock over them. Steam on the 2nd rail of the steamer for 11 minutes at 100 °. After 6 minutes of cooking time, mix the mussels well with a wooden spoon or remove the cooking tray and shake vigorously. Serve with white bread.

20. Citrus and herb sea bass

177 kcal

Ingredients for 4 servings:
- ∴ 4 skinless *sea bass* fillets
- ∴ 3 tbsp *lemon peel*
- ∴ 3 tbsp *orange peel*
- ∴ 1 tbsp *lemon juice*
- ∴ 4 tbsp *orange juice*
- ∴ 1/2 teaspoon *ginger* salt
- ∴ 1 bunch of herbs
- ∴ *herbal* salt

Season the sea bass fillets with herb salt and cook in a closed container for 10 minutes at 80 °. Wash the fresh herbs, shake dry and chop finely. Mix the herbs with the lemon peel and the orange peel. Place each fish fillet on a preheated plate, sprinkle with ginger salt and herb mixture and pour orange juice over it.

Enjoyable alternative: sauté the herb mixture with 50g butter in a pan. Add 130g breadcrumbs and toast briefly. Spread the crumb and herb mixture on the fish fillets.

Flesh

Meat dishes should be on the table at least once a week and with every Sunday meal. Delicious dishes with chicken, beef, pork, turkey and the like can also be conjured up in the steamer, nutritious and rich in vitamins. The simple preparation will convince you.

A little tip for preparing meat dishes in the steam cooker: If you prefer roasted aromas, fry the meat briefly before cooking it.

1. Tafelspitz - a kitchen classic for the Sunday table

223 kcal

Ingredients for 4 servings:
- ∴ *750g beef*
- ∴ *1 bunch of soup greens*
- ∴ *2 small onions*
- ∴ *1 small* stick of *leek*
- ∴ *1 clove of garlic*
- ∴ *1 bay leaf*
- ∴ *1* teaspoon *juniper berries*
- ∴ *1* tsp *allspice grains*

∴ *1 sprig of lovage*

∴ *thyme*

∴ *1 bunch of parsley*

∴ *2 carrots*

∴ *1 zucchini*

∴ *salt, pepper*

Wash, clean and chop the soup greens. Peel and chop the onions. Peel and roughly mash the garlic. Put all the chopped ingredients in a cooking tray without holes. Add the thyme, bay leaves, allspice grains and juniper berries. Remove the tendons and skins from the beef, season with salt and pepper. Place the beef with the other ingredients in the steamer. Cook in its own juice for 90 minutes at 90 °.

In the meantime, wash the remaining carrots, leek and courgette, peel and cut into strips if necessary. Season lightly with salt, pepper and thyme. Chop the parsley and add to the vegetables. Cook everything in a perforated basket for 12 minutes.

Arrange the boiled beef with the vegetables on preheated plates. Save the beef broth from the cooking container, it can be used for a hearty soup or sauce! Boiled potatoes go best with this.

2. Sliced turkey with mushroom sauce

384 kcal

Ingredients for 4 servings:
- ∴ *600g turkey schnitzel*
- ∴ *300ml white wine*
- ∴ *1 small red onion*
- ∴ *300g mushrooms (mushrooms,* king *oyster mushrooms)*
- ∴ *150ml cream*
- ∴ *1* tbsp *flour*
- ∴ *1* tbsp *chopped parsley*
- ∴ *1* tbsp *chopped chives*
- ∴ *2* tbsp *olive oil*
- ∴ *salt, pepper*

Wash turkey meat, pat dry and cut into cubes. Pepper and salt and place in the closed steamer. Mix the white wine with the flour and pour over the turkey meat. Cook for 15 minutes at 90 °. Chop the onion and parsley, slice the mushrooms and fry everything in a little hot olive oil. Deglaze with cream. Pour the mushroom sauce over the schnitzel and steam again for 3 minutes. Serve sprinkled with chopped chives. This goes well with rice or pasta.

3. Beef roulades with ribbon noodles - perfect for Sunday lunch

490 kcal

Ingredients for 4 servings:
- ∴ *4 beef roulades*
- ∴ *8 pickles*
- ∴ *4 carrots*
- ∴ *1* teaspoon *mustard*
- ∴ *4 slices of bacon*
- ∴ *300g ribbon noodles*
- ∴ *500ml water*
- ∴ *1 bunch of soup vegetables*
- ∴ *1 onion*
- ∴ *150ml beef broth*
- ∴ *200ml water*
- ∴ *100ml dry red wine*
- ∴ *1* tbsp *cold butter*

Salt and pepper the beef roulades and spread a thin layer of mustard. Cut the pickles into strips. Peel the carrots and cut into strips. Place a slice of smoked ham on each roulade. Spread the pickles and carrots on the roulades and roll up each roulade tightly and secure with toothpicks or meat skewers. Fry the roulades briefly on all sides in a little oil in a hot pan. Wash, clean and chop soup vegetables. Peel the onion and cut into strips. Put the vegetables, onions and roulades in a closed steamer. Pour in the stock and water and cook everything for 60 minutes at 90 °. In the meantime, place the tagliatelle in another closed steamer, add 500ml water and steam for 20 minutes at 100 °. Take the roulades out of the container. Pour the liquid off into a saucepan, strain the vegetables through a sieve. Season the sauce with salt, pepper and red wine. Bring to the boil once, assemble in flakes with cold butter.

Arrange the tagliatelle on a plate, spread the roulades over it, pour the sauce over everything and serve.

4. Beef schnitzel with roasted potatoes

411 kcal

Ingredients for 4 servings:
- ∴ *4 beef* schnitzel
- ∴ *400g potatoes*
- ∴ *550ml water*
- ∴ *1* teaspoon *mustard*
- ∴ *salt, pepper*

Salt and pepper the beef schnitzel and coat both sides with mustard. Steam in the perforated steamer for 45 minutes at 90 °. Peel and dice the potatoes. Place in a closed container and pour the water over them. Steam for 20 minutes at 100 °. Sear the steamed potatoes in a pan without oil, season with salt and pepper. Arrange the meat and potatoes on preheated plates. A crunchy leaf salad goes well with it.

5. Turkey roulade with spinach

361 kcal

Ingredients for 4 servings:
- ∴ *4 turkey* schnitzel
- ∴ *500g spinach* leaves
- ∴ *120g sheep cheese*
- ∴ *2 cloves of garlic*
- ∴ *salt, pepper*

Wash and sort the spinach leaves and steam in the perforated steamer for 3 minutes at 100 °. Peel garlic and chop finely. Salt and pepper the spinach and mix in the chopped garlic. Dice the sheep cheese and stir into the spinach. Salt and pepper the turkey schnitzel and brush with the spinach mixture. Roll up the schnitzel tightly and secure with toothpicks. If you want toasted flavors, sear the turkey roulades in a very hot pan with little fat all around for 1 minute, then place in the perforated container and let steam at 90 ° for 19 minutes.

Tip: In spring, when there is fresh wild garlic again, replace the spinach with (1-2 bunches) wild garlic. The wild garlic does not have to be steamed separately!

6. Herb schnitzel

256 kcal

Ingredients for 4 servings:
  ∴ *4 turkey* schnitzel
  ∴ *1 bunch of parsley*
  ∴ *1 bunch of chives*
  ∴ *1/2 lemon*

Wash turkey schnitzel and pat dry. Sear them in a hot pan with a little oil for a maximum of 30 seconds. Put the schnitzel in the perforated steamer and cook for 20 minutes at 90 °. Meanwhile wash the herbs, shake dry and finely chop. Squeeze the lemon and mix the juice with the herbs. Press the finished schnitzel into the herb mixture and serve.

It goes well with brown rice and a fresh cucumber salad.

7. Chicken "Asia" - very exotic

142 kcal

Ingredients for 4 servings:
- ∴ *500g chicken*
- ∴ *1* pk. *Asian vegetable mix*
- ∴ *5* tbsp *soy sauce*
- ∴ *salt, pepper*

Wash the chicken, pat dry and cut into small pieces. Season with salt, pepper and soy sauce and cook in the closed steamer for 15 minutes at 85 °. Let the vegetables thaw briefly, season with the remaining soy sauce and cook in the perforated container for 15 minutes at 100 °. Mix the meat and vegetables, season with salt, pepper and soy sauce. Rice is ideal as a side dish.

8. Minute steaks with green vegetables - a quick lunch

332 kcal

Ingredients for 4 servings:
- ∴ *400g minute steaks*
- ∴ *150g sugar* snap *peas*

∴ *300g Brussels sprouts*

∴ *300g broccoli*

∴ *1 clove of garlic*

∴ *125ml vegetable stock*

∴ *250g cream cheese*

∴ *1 shot of white wine*

∴ *oil*

∴ *salt, pepper*

Wash the broccoli and cut into bite-sized florets. Clean and halve the sugar snap peas. Wash and clean Brussels sprouts and cut crosswise on the stalk. Put the vegetables in the perforated steamer and cook for 7 minutes at 100 °. In the meantime, wash the minute steaks, pat dry, season with salt and pepper. Sear them in a little oil in a hot pan on both sides. Peel the garlic and press it through the garlic press into the pan. Fry briefly, deglaze with white wine and stock. Add the cream cheese and stir well. Add the steamed vegetables and season with salt and pepper. Briefly put in the minute steaks and simmer for about 2 minutes.

9. Stuffed chicken rolls with herb salad

528 kcal

Ingredients for 4 servings:

∴. *4 chicken breast* fillets

∴. *1 bunch of rocket*

∴. *1/2 endive*

∴. *1 onion*

∴. *100g sheep cheese*

∴. *1 bunch of fresh herbs*

∴. *1/2 lettuce*

∴. *1 head of radicchio*

∴. *8 slices of Serrano ham*

∴. *2* tbsp *olive oil*

∴. *3* tbsp *balsamic vinegar*

∴. *1/2* teaspoon *chopped rosemary*

∴. *lemon juice*

∴. *salt, pepper*

Wash the chicken breasts, pat dry using the "butterfly cut" cut into large, flat pieces, season with salt and pepper. Wash the rocket, shake dry and roughly chop. Peel the onion and cut into fine pieces. Crumble the sheep cheese. Mix the sheep cheese with rosemary, onion and rocket, drizzle everything with lemon juice. Spread the sheep cheese mixture on the chicken breasts and roll them up tightly. Wrap each roll with 2 slices of ham. Cook in the perforated steamer for 20 minutes at 90 °.

Meanwhile, for the herb salad, wash the radicchio, endive and lettuce and cut roughly. Wash the herbs, shake dry and finely chop and mix with olive oil and balsamic vinegar to form a marinade. Season to taste with salt and pepper. Marinate the salad just before serving.

10. Far Eastern Chicken - with lots of spices for an exotic aroma

415 kcal

Ingredients for 4 servings:

∴ *4 chicken breast* fillets

∴ *1 zucchini*

∴ *2 tomatoes*

∴ *1 red onion*

∴ *1 carrot*

∴ *1* tbsp *raisins*

∴ *1 piece of ginger (approx. 1/2 cm)*

∴ *1 clove of garlic*

∴ *200ml chicken soup*

∴ *1* teaspoon *curry powder*

∴ *1* teaspoon cornstarch

Chilli ∴ *flakes as desired*

∴ *salt*

Wash the chicken breast fillets, pat dry and cut into strips. Peel the onion and cut into wedges. Wash tomatoes, zucchini and carrots and cut into slices or cubes. Put everything in the perforated steamer and season with salt. Pour the chicken soup over them. Peel and crush the garlic clove. Peel and chop the ginger. Add everything to the chicken. Stir in the curry, chilli flakes, cornstarch and raisins. Cook for 15 minutes at 100 °. Season to taste with curry, chilli flakes and salt.

Rice goes well with it.

11. Steamed meat - easy preparation and a quick meal

229 kcal

Ingredients for 4 servings:
        ∴ *750g pork* loin
        ∴ *2 cloves of garlic*
        ∴ *1* teaspoon *thyme*
        ∴ *1* teaspoon *caraway seeds*
        ∴ *125ml water*
        ∴ *salt*

Wash pork and pat dry, rub well with all the spices. Fill a closed steam container finger-high with water and place the meat in it. Steam for 20 minutes at 90 °, dousing the juice more often.

Boiled potatoes and salad go well as a side dish.

12. Chicken breast wrapped in chard

443 kcal

Ingredients for 4 servings:
∴ *4 chicken breasts*
∴ *8 leaves of* Swiss *chard*
∴ *1 white onion*
∴ *1 red* pepper
∴ *100g ricotta*
∴ *50g mountain cheese*
∴ *250ml chicken stock*
∴ *4* tbsp *sherry*
∴ *8 leaves of basil*
∴ *salt, pepper*

Wash the chard leaves and blanch in boiling salted water for 1 minute, rinse ice-cold. Peel and finely chop the onion. Wash and finely chop the peppers. Wash the basil leaves, shake dry and finely chop. Mix the paprika, basil ricotta and mountain cheese, season with salt and pepper. Lay out the chard leaves, overlapping in pairs, and brush with the mixture. Salt and pepper the chicken, place on the chard leaves and wrap.

Cook the chard parcels in a steamer for 20 minutes at 90 °. Mix the sherry with the poultry stock and bring to the boil. Serve the chicken breasts with the sherry brew.

13. Beef fillet in an herb coating - Highlight for the festive table

90 kcal

Ingredients for 4 servings:
- *∴ 400g beef fillet*
- *∴ 2 tbsp mustard*
- *∴ 2 bunch of herbs of your choice*
- *∴ salt, pepper*

Clean, wash and pat dry the beef fillet. Rub with mustard, salt and pepper. Cook in the steamer for 10 minutes at 90 °. In the meantime, wash the herbs, pat dry and finely chop them. Turn the hot beef fillet in the herbs, wrap in heat-resistant foil and let cool down a little. Cut into thin slices with a sharp knife.

14. Lamb shoulder with couscous - an oriental pleasure

817 kcal

Ingredients for 4 servings:

∴ *800g shoulder of lamb*

∴ *350g couscous*

∴ *80g whole almonds*

∴ *80g dates*

∴ *70g raisins*

∴ *5g harissa paste*

∴ *1 red pepper*

∴ *1 eggplant*

∴ *1 zucchini*

∴ *1 large onion*

∴ *1 bunch of mint*

∴ *salt, pepper*

Wash the zucchini, aubergine and bell pepper and cut into bite-sized pieces.

Core and halve the dates. Place the vegetables, dates and almonds in a closed steamer insert, season with salt and pepper. Cut the lamb shoulder, rub with salt and pepper and place on the vegetables. Cook everything for 120 minutes at 100 °. Bring the couscous to the boil and soak in warm water. Mix with harissa, picked mint leaves, raisins and salt. Place the lamb shoulder on a bed of couscous and vegetables and garnish with mint leaves.

15. Steamed veal fillet - a poem with chervil

425 kcal

Ingredients for 4 servings:
- ∴ *4 veal fillets á 140g*
- ∴ *200g sugar* snap *peas*
- ∴ *1 bunch of chervil*
- ∴ *2 shallots*
- ∴ *20g butter*
- ∴ *3* tbsp *dry vermouth*
- ∴ *175g soy cream*
- ∴ *1* teaspoon *oil*
- ∴ *salt, pepper*

Peel and finely dice shallots. Wash the sugar snap peas and cut into fine strips. Wash chervil, shake dry. Finely chop half and pluck the leaves from the other half. Wash the veal fillets, pat dry, season with salt and pepper. Sear in a pan over high heat for 30 seconds. Put the chervil leaves in a perforated steamer, place the meat on top and cover with the sugar snap peas strips. Finish cooking the meat for 6 minutes at 90 °. Froth the butter in a pan, sauté the shallot cubes until colorless. Deglaze with vermouth and let it boil down completely. Add the soy cream, bring to the boil and reduce until creamy at a reduced temperature. Stir in the chopped chervil, season with salt and pepper. Serve the meat with the vegetables and sauce.

16. Butter-tender beef stew

356 kcal

Ingredients for 4 servings:
- ∴ *1000g roast beef*
- ∴ *4 carrots*
- ∴ *1 celery* bulb
- ∴ *100g mushrooms*
- ∴ *1 large onion*
- ∴ *3 cloves of garlic*
- ∴ *100ml red wine*
- ∴ *200ml meat* stock
- ∴ *2 sprigs of rosemary*
- ∴ *4 sprigs of thyme*
- ∴ *10 leaves of sage*
- ∴ *salt, pepper*

Briefly sear the beef in a very hot pan on each side. Put in a steamer. Peel the carrots, peel the celery and cut both into long strips. Peel and halve the onion. Peel and halve the garlic. Clean the mushrooms and cut in half. Peel the carrots and celery and cut into long strips. Halve the onion and garlic clove. Halve the mushrooms. Spread everything around the roast beef. Add red wine and meat stock. Roughly chop all herbs and add them, salt and pepper. Cook for 120 minutes at 100 °.

Serve with mashed potatoes and salad.

17. Pollo Rosso - a delicious main course that tastes like a holiday!

453 kcal

Ingredients for 4 servings:
- ∴ *600g chicken breast*
- ∴ *500g tomatoes*
- ∴ *6 black olives*
- ∴ 2 tbsp *herbs (basil, parsley)*
- ∴ *1 clove of garlic*
- ∴ *salt, pepper*

Rub the chicken breast with salt and pepper and place in the closed steamer. Wash, peel and puree the tomatoes. Wash herbs, shake dry and chop. Peel and chop the garlic. Mix the herbs, garlic and tomatoes and pour over the chicken. Stone the olives, cut into rings and sprinkle over them. Cook everything for 20 minutes at 90 °. It goes well with flatbread or baguette.

18. Paprika goulash - nutritious and filling, just right on cold days!

312 kcal

Ingredients for 4 servings:
- ∴ *600g beef from the calf or shoulder*
- ∴ *400g onion*
- ∴ *300ml water*
- ∴ *200mml dark beer*
- ∴ 2 teaspoons of *tomato paste*
- ∴ 2 teaspoons of *brown sugar*
- ∴ *1 teaspoon whole caraway seeds*
- ∴ *1 teaspoon ground pepper*
- ∴ 1 teaspoon sweet *paprika powder*
- ∴ *1 tbsp butter*
- ∴ *1 tbsp flour*
- ∴ *1 tbsp oil*
- ∴ *1 lemon*
- ∴ *salt*

Peel and roughly dice the onions. Wash and peel the lemon. Finely chop the caraway seeds with the lemon zest and butter. The butter is only needed to keep the caraway from jumping off. Season the goulash with salt and sugar. Roast the onion cubes in oil, stir in the cumin and lemon butter, paprika powder, salt, tomato paste and brown sugar. Add the meat cubes and fry vigorously. First with beer, then gradually deglaze with water and fill up. Put the goulash in a closed steamer and cook for about 120 minutes at 100 °.

Dumplings or fresh bread go well with this!

19. Bohemian beer meat

632 kcal

Ingredients for 4 servings:
- ∴ *1000g shoulder pork*
- ∴ *100g butter*
- ∴ *1/2 l beer*
- ∴ *1* teaspoon of *ground caraway seeds*
- ∴ *3* tbsp *black bread, ground into crumbs*
- ∴ *salt, pepper*

Wash the pork, pat dry and cut into cubes. Sear them in melted butter, season with salt, pepper and sprinkle with caraway seeds. Mix well and pour on the beer. Place in a closed steamer and cook for 45 minutes at 100 °. Add the black bread crumbs and cook for another 20 minutes. Bread dumplings go well with it.

20. Chicken paprika

- the so-called paprika chicken is a popular dish in Austria and very typical of Austrian cuisine. It is traditionally served with napkin dumplings or corn grits (Turkish sterz or Turkish pudding).

614 kcal

Ingredients for 4 servings:

∴ *1 whole chicken*

∴ *2 onions*

∴ *2* tbsp *butter*

∴ *2 cloves of garlic*

∴ *2* teaspoons of *paprika powder*

∴ *1/8 l white wine*

∴ *2* teaspoons of cornstarch

∴ *2* tbsp *sour cream*

∴ *chicken soup*

∴ *marjoram*

∴ *salt, pepper*

Wash the chicken, pat dry and cut into pieces. Fry the poultry parts quickly in hot butter and keep warm. Peel and dice the onions and roast them in the frying fat. Peel and mash the garlic. Add the garlic and paprika powder to the onions and roast briefly. Pour white wine and chicken soup on top. Put the stock in the closed steamer, add the pieces of meat and cook for 40 minutes at 100 °. Remove the chicken from the container, remove the skin and bones. Mix the sour cream with the cornstarch and use it to thicken the sauce. Season with salt, pepper and marjoram, put the meat in the sauce and bring to the boil.

Side dishes and vegetarian dishes

Vegetables are easy to prepare in the steamer and keep their color. But dumplings, pasta and other side dishes also work well under steam. Here you will find classic side dishes such as bread dumplings, but also unusual dishes such as Austrian Turkish pudding.

1. Vegetable lasagna - vegetarian and tastes good anyway.

407 kcal

Ingredients for 4 servings:
∴ *2 small zucchini*
∴ *1 carrot*
∴ *1* spring *onion*
∴ *15 sheets of lasagne*

350g∴ sliced mozzarella

∴ 120g grated parmesan cheese

∴ 1 glass of tomato sugo

∴ 1 tbsp *olive oil*

∴ pepper

Wash, peel and dice the zucchini and carrots. Chop the spring onion into fine rings. Brush the closed steamer container with olive oil and cover the bottom with lasagne sheets. Spread about 1/3 of the tomato sauce on top, cover with 1/3 of the vegetables. Place half of the mozzarella slices on top. Place the next layer of lasagne sheets on top and do the same. Finally sprinkle with grated parmesan and pepper. Cook for 35 minutes at 100 °.

2. Turkish pudding

343 kcal

Ingredients for 4 servings:

750ml∴ milk

∴ 150g corn semolina

∴ 3 eggs

∴ 50g cheese

∴ nutmeg

∴ salt

Bring the milk to the boil and slowly pour in the corn semolina. Reduce to a thick paste while stirring constantly. Take the pot off the stove and let the mixture cool down. Separate eggs. Rasp cheese. Stir egg yolk, cheese and nutmeg into the cold semolina mass. Beat egg whites until stiff and fold in. Place in a closed steamer and cook for approx. 60 minutes at 100 °.

The Turkish pudding is traditionally served with chicken in Austria, but goes well with all stew dishes with a lot of sauce.

3. Tomato Gnocchi

218 kcal

Ingredients for 4 servings:
- ∴ *500g* floury *potatoes*
- ∴ *60g flour*
- ∴ *40g potato starch*
- ∴ *3* tbsp *tomato paste*
- ∴ *1* tbsp *butter*
- ∴ *1 egg*
- ∴ *50g dried tomatoes*
- ∴ *1* tbsp *olive oil*

∴ *salt*

Wash the potatoes and cook in the closed steamer for 30 minutes at 100 ° until soft. Finely chop the sun-dried tomatoes and pour olive oil over them in a bowl. Peel the soft-cooked potatoes while they are still hot and grate them finely. Mix with all remaining ingredients and knead into a dough. If the dough is too soft, add a little more flour. Shape the dough into rolls approx. 1 cm thick and flatten a little with a fork. Cut into small pieces. Cook the dough pieces in the closed steamer for 10 minutes at 100 °.

4. Spinach and sheep cheese lasagna

330 kcal

Ingredients for 4 servings:
    ∴ *400g spinach leaves (frozen goods)*
    ∴ *250g sheep cheese*
    ∴ *1 pack of lasagne sheets*
    ∴ *250g sour cream*
    ∴ *1 small onion*
    ∴ *2 cloves of garlic*
    ∴ 2 tablespoons of *chopped parsley*
    ∴ *2 eggs*

∴ salt, pepper

Thaw spinach leaves and roughly chop. Keep the spinach juice, it is needed for cooking. Peel and finely chop the onion, peel and press the garlic. Mix the spinach with the onion, garlic, parsley, sour cream and eggs. Salt and pepper. Crumble the sheep cheese and mix 3/4 of it into the spinach mixture. Brush the closed steamer container with oil and cover with a layer of lasagne sheets. Spread 1/3 of the spinach mixture on top, cover with lasagne sheets and again cover with another third of the spinach mixture. Keep doing this until there is no spinach left. Spread the remaining sheep cheese on the last layer of spinach. Steam for 25-30 minutes at 100 ° C.

5. Napkin dumplings

- the classic among the side dishes goes well with almost all meat dishes. With mushroom sauce and green salad, the hearty, tender napkin dumplings are also a filling main course.

227 kcal

Ingredients for 4 servings:
    ∴ 1 baguette
    ∴ 250ml milk

∴ 1 onion

∴ 1 bunch of parsley

∴ 3 eggs

∴ 2 teaspoons of *anise*

∴ *nutmeg*

∴ *salt*

Cut the baguette into cubes. Peel and chop the onion, fry in butter until golden brown. Warm the milk and pour it over the bread cubes. Add onion cubes and eggs. Wash parsley, shake dry and finely chop. Mix into the bread mixture. Season the dumpling dough with anise, nutmeg and salt, shape into a smooth, even roll and wrap in cling film. Cook for 30 minutes at 100 °. Cut the finished dumpling into 2cm thick slices and serve.

6. Swiss potato dumplings

393 kcal

Ingredients for 4 servings:

∴ *1000g potatoes*

∴ *60g cheese*

∴ *1 onion*

∴ *330ml milk*

∴ *4 tbsp flour*

∴ *4 tbsp butter*

∴ *salt*

Peel the onion, cut into rings and roast in 1 tbsp butter. Cook the potatoes for 30 minutes at 100 °. Peel while hot and press through the potato press. Mix the flour in the cold milk and bring to the boil, stirring constantly with a whisk. Salt the milk and mix with the mashed potatoes. Spread butter on a closed steamer. Melt the rest of the butter. Cut out cams from the dough with a spoon and layer them in the container. Dip the spoon in hot butter in between. Spread the onion rings on the cam. Grate cheese and sprinkle over it. Cook in the steamer for 10 minutes at 100 ° until the cheese has melted. If you prefer browned cheese, you can bake the cams at 180 ° top / bottom heat in the oven. The potato dumplings taste great as an accompaniment to meat and sauces, but also on their own with a green salad.

7. Potato noodles

231 kcal

Ingredients for 4 servings:
∴ *700g potatoes*
∴ *8* tbsp whole *wheat flour*
∴ *2 eggs*
∴ *nutmeg*

∴ salt

Cook the potatoes in the perforated steamer for 25 minutes at 100 °. Peel while hot and press through the potato press. Add eggs and flour to the potatoes, season the dough with nutmeg and salt. Shape a roll and cut it into small pieces. Use it to form noodles as thick as a finger. Place the pasta in the perforated container of the steamer and steam for 15 minutes at 100 °.

8. Stewed cucumbers

109 kcal

Ingredients for 4 servings:
- ∴ *150g cucumber*
- ∴ *500g potatoes*
- ∴ *70ml low-fat yogurt*
- ∴ *100ml vegetable stock*
- ∴ *1 bunch of dill*
- ∴ *salt, pepper*

Peel and halve the cucumber and scrape out the core with a small spoon. Dice the cucumber. Peel and dice the potatoes. Place the cucumber and potatoes in the closed steamer, season with salt and pepper. Wash dill, shake dry and finely chop. Mix with the cucumber and potatoes. Pour in the vegetable stock and cook everything for 20 minutes at 100 °. Pour off the juice, mix with the yoghurt and mix back with the vegetables. Rice or wholemeal bread tastes good with it.

9. Ham pasta - a simple, quick dinner

1056 kcal

Ingredients for 4 servings:
  ∴ *500g Farfalle*
  ∴ *600g cream*
  ∴ *500ml vegetable stock*
  ∴ *400ml ham*
  ∴ *herbs at will*
  ∴ *salt*

Dice the ham. Mix all ingredients in the closed steamer. Cook for 20 minutes at 100 °, stirring occasionally. Season to taste with salt and chopped herbs before serving.

10. Saffron rice with broccoli

334 kcal

Ingredients for 4 servings:
  ∴ *300g rice*

∴ *720ml water*

∴ *500g broccoli*

∴ 2 pk *saffron threads*

∴ *1* teaspoon *ground cardamom*

∴ *2* tablespoons of *oil*

∴ *1* teaspoon *salt*

Steam rice in hot oil until translucent. Pour water on, add salt, cardamom and saffron threads and cook everything in the closed steamer for 20 minutes at 100 °. Wash the broccoli, cut into florets and cook in the steamer for 18 minutes at 100 ° until al dente. Mix the broccoli with the rice and serve.

11. Russian manti

83 kcal

Ingredients for 4 servings:

∴ *600g mixed minced meat*

∴ *3 onions*

∴ *30ml sunflower oil*

∴ *salt, pepper*

For the dough:

∴ *600g flour*

∴ *1-2 egg (s)*

∴ *330ml lukewarm water*

∴ *salt*

Make a firm pasta dough from water, flour, eggs and salt, shape into a ball, sprinkle with flour and cover for approx. 30 minutes.

For the filling, peel and chop the onion and work it with the minced meat to form an even mass. Mix in the oil, salt and pepper.

Knead the dough and divide it into 8 equal pieces. Roll out each piece into a 3-4mm thick circle, cut out squares. Put 1 tablespoon of minced meat filling on each square of dough. Fold in the two opposite corners and press together. Press the sides together. Brush each manti with oil and place in the sieve inserts of the steamer. Stack the sieve inserts in the steamer, cook for 45-50 minutes at 100 °. Take out the mantis one by one and serve immediately. In Russia you eat it with sour cream and flatbread.

12. Rocket risotto

442 kcal

Ingredients for 4 servings:

∴ 250g risotto rice

∴ 1 bunch of rocket

∴ 100g grated parmesan cheese

∴ 650ml vegetable stock

∴ 150ml white wine

∴ 1 onion

∴ 2 tbsp olive oil

∴ 1 tbsp butter

∴ 1 tbsp chopped parsley

∴ salt, pepper

Peel and chop the onion and sauté with the chopped parsley in olive oil until translucent. Put the rice in the closed steamer, mix with the onion mixture, white wine and vegetable stock. Cook for 20 minutes at 100 °. Wash the rocket, shake dry and cut into coarse strips and mix with the rice 5 minutes before the end of the cooking time. If necessary, add a little more soup. Season the risotto with salt and pepper and refine with butter and grated parmesan.

13. Romanesco with ham and cheese sauce - a quick and savory lunch.

109 kcal

Ingredients for 4 persons:

∴ *1-2 heads of Romanesco*

∴ *8 slices of ham*

∴ *250ml milk*

∴ *100g cheese*

∴ *8 corners of processed cheese*

∴ *nutmeg*

∴ *salt, pepper*

Divide the romanesco into florets, wash, salt and cook for 19 minutes at 100 ° until al dente. In the meantime, warm up the milk. Cut the cheese into small cubes and add to the milk with the processed cheese wedges. Bring to the boil and stir until the cheese has dissolved
Season with pepper and nutmeg.

Cut the ham into strips, stir half of them into the cheese sauce. Spread the romanesco on plates, pour the ham and cheese sauce on top and sprinkle with the remaining strips of ham.

14. Risi Bisi - very popular with children

318 kcal

Ingredients for 4 servings:

∴ *1 cup of rice*

∴ *400g chicken*

∴ *2 cups of water*

∴ *300g peas*

∴ *salt, pepper*

Put rice in the rice container of the steamer, add water and steam for 20 minutes at 100 °. Peel fresh peas, defrost frozen peas, drain canned peas. Cook the peas in the perforated steamer for 20 minutes at 100 °. Wash the chicken, pat dry and cut into bite-sized pieces. Salt and pepper and cook for 15 minutes at 85 °. Mix the peas with the cooked rice and season with salt. Arrange the meat with the rice and serve.

15. Rice dish - a simple dinner

355 kcal

Ingredients for 4 servings:

∴ *1 cup of* basmati *rice*

∴ *11/2 cups of water*

∴ *4 eggs*

∴ *200g herder cheese*

∴ *4 teaspoons of herbs*

∴ *salt*

Cook the rice and water in the closed steamer for 15 minutes at

100 °. Wash herbs, shake dry and finely chop. Put rice, cheese, herbs and eggs in a pan. Fry over high heat, stirring constantly.

16. Rice pancakes - a sweet dinner and therefore popular with children.

100 kcal

Ingredients for 4 servings:
- ∴ *3* tbsp *rice flour*
- ∴ *11/2* tbsp *brown sugar*
- ∴ *1 egg*
- ∴ *200g natural yogurt*
- ∴ *1/5* pack of *baking powder*

Mix all ingredients well in a bowl. Cook in the closed steamer for 20 minutes at 100 °. Sprinkle with icing sugar and serve with applesauce.

17. Ratatouille - a classic insert, and not just since the cartoon of the same name.

97 kcal

Ingredients for 4 servings:
- ∴ *4 tomatoes*

∴ 1 onion

∴ 2 cloves of garlic

∴ 1 bell pepper

∴ 1 zucchini

∴ 2 tbsp *olive oil*

∴ 1 tbsp *thyme*

∴ 1 dash of tomato juice

∴ 1 teaspoon *salt*

∴ *pepper*

Wash the tomatoes, onions and zucchini thoroughly and dice them with a good cutting knife. Wash and core the peppers and cut into strips. Peel the garlic and cut into small pieces. Put all ingredients in the closed steamer, drizzle with olive oil, season with salt and pepper. Cook for 20 minutes at around 90 °. Finely chop the thyme. Season the finished ratatouille with salt and pepper, mix with chopped thyme and a dash of tomato juice.

18. Pasta with spinach leaves

720 kcal

Ingredients for 4 servings:
∴ *550g spaghetti*
∴ *800g spinach leaves*

∴ *350g cocktail tomatoes*

∴ *2 onions*

∴ *1 cup of sour cream*

∴ 4 tbsp *parmesan*

∴ *salt, pepper*

Cook the spaghetti in salted water until al dente. Wash and clean the spinach leaves and place in the closed steamer. Peel and finely chop the onion and spread over the spinach. Salt and pepper and steam for 12 minutes at 100 °. Wash tomatoes, cut in half and steam for 5 minutes at 100 °. Mix the spinach, tomatoes and sour cream, season with salt and pepper. Grate the parmesan. Turn the spaghetti in the spinach sauce and serve sprinkled with parmesan.

19. Paella

541 kcal

Ingredients for 4 servings:

∴ *300g rice*

∴ *500g chicken*

∴ *1/2 l chicken soup*

∴ *2 peppers*

∴ *200g peas*

∴ *200g broccoli*

∴ *2 onions*

∴ 2 tbsp *soy sauce*

∴ 2 tbsp *saffron*

∴ *salt, pepper*

Peel onions and cut them into fine pieces. Braise in oil with rice and saffron.

Deglaze rice with chicken soup, steam in the rice container of the steamer for 30 minutes at 100 °. Wash the bell peppers, remove the core and cut into strips. Wash broccoli and cut into florets. Steam the broccoli, bell pepper and peas in a second steamer for 15 minutes at 100 °. Wash the chicken, pat dry, cut into bite-sized pieces and season with salt and pepper.

Fry the chicken pieces and deglaze with soy sauce. Steam on the cooking plate of the steamer for 20 minutes at 85 °. Mix all ingredients together, season with salt and pepper and serve.

20. Pumpkin risotto

485 kcal

Ingredients for 4 servings:

∴ *250g risotto rice*

∴ *350g pumpkin*

∴ *1 onion*

∴ *150g grated parmesan cheese*

∴ *1/4 l white wine*

∴ *1 l vegetable* stock

∴ *1* teaspoon *butter*

∴ *pepper*

Put the rice in the closed steamer or in a special rice container, add the wine, season with salt and pepper. Peel onions and cut them into fine pieces. Add to the rice and cook everything for 4 minutes at 100 °. Pour in half of the vegetable stock, cook for another 8 minutes. Peel the pumpkin, cut into cubes and cook in the perforated container for 10 minutes at 100 °. Stir the rice, pour in the rest of the bouillon. Finely puree half of the pumpkin cubes with the hand blender, mix the puree with the remaining pumpkin cubes into the risotto. Refine with butter and parmesan.

21. Pumpkin cream soup

66 kcal

Ingredients for 4 servings:

∴ *500g pumpkin*

∴ *1 large, floury potato*

∴ *1 clove of garlic*

105

∴ *1 small onion*

∴ *1 liter of water*

∴ *1 soup cube*

∴ 3 tbsp heavy *cream*

∴ 1 tbsp *creme fraiche*

∴ *1 piece of ginger*

∴ *salt, pepper*

Peel the pumpkin, remove the seeds, dice the pumpkin flesh. Peel and dice the potato. Peel onion and chop finely. Peel and press the garlic. Put the onion, garlic, pumpkin and potato in the closed steamer, fill up with 1 liter of water. Season to taste with the soup cube, salt and pepper. Peel and grate the ginger, add to the pumpkin soup. Cook the pumpkin soup for 15 minutes at 100 degrees and then puree with a blender. Add the cream and creme fraiche, stir and, if necessary, season again with salt and pepper.

22. Cabbage rolls

503 kcal

Ingredients for 4 servings:

∴ *1 head of* cabbage

∴ *500g minced meat mixed*

∴ *2 onions*

∴ *150g rice*

∴ *1 egg*

∴ *1* pack of *pureed tomatoes*

∴ *1* tbsp *soft butter*

∴ *1* tbsp *chopped parsley*

∴ *1* tbsp *herbs*

∴ *oil*

∴ *salt, pepper*

Cook the rice until soft. Peel 16 large leaves from the cabbage, remove the stalk and blanch in hot water until they are easily pliable. Take out, rinse in cold water and pat dry. Peel onions and cut them into fine pieces. Knead the onion, minced meat, parsley, egg, boiled rice, butter, salt and pepper well until you get a homogeneous mixture. Always put two cabbage leaves together and cover with minced meat mixture. Knock in on the side, roll up and fix with toothpicks. Cook in the steamer for 20 minutes at 100 °. Meanwhile, for the tomato sauce, put the pureed tomatoes with the mixed herbs, salt and pepper in a saucepan, bring to the boil and simmer gently. Serve the cabbage rolls with the tomato sauce. Boiled potatoes go well with it.

23. Kohlrabi ragout

174 kcal

Ingredients for 4 servings:
- ∴ *4 kohlrabi*
- ∴ *800g potatoes*
- ∴ *100ml vegetable stock*
- ∴ *5 tbsp low-fat yogurt*
- ∴ *1* tbsp *caraway seeds*
- ∴ *2* tbsp *chervil*
- ∴ *1 dash of vinegar*
- ∴ *nutmeg*
- ∴ *salt, pepper*

Wash the potatoes and cook with the skin in the perforated steamer for 30 minutes at 100 °. Peel the kohlrabi, cut into thin strips and mix in the closed steamer with the vegetable stock, a little vinegar, salt, pepper, nutmeg and caraway seeds. Steam for 25 minutes at 100 °. Wash the chervil, shake dry and finely chop. Stir in the kohlrabi. Finally stir in yogurt and serve with the jacket potatoes.

24. Potato soup - enjoyable and tasty

175 kcal

Ingredients for 4 servings:

∴ *500g potatoes*

∴ *2 carrots*

∴ *1/2 l vegetable* stock

∴ *3* tbsp heavy *cream*

∴ *200g mixed mushrooms*

∴ *1 clove of garlic*

∴ *1 small onion*

∴ *marjoram*

∴ *salt, pepper*

Potatoes and peel and cut into small cubes. Peel and chop the onion and garlic. Wash and peel the carrots. Clean the mushrooms and cut them into leaves. Put the potatoes, whole carrots, onions, garlic, spices and mushrooms in the closed cooking basket and steam for 30-35 minutes at 100 °. Remove the carrots from the soup. Puree the potato soup finely, refine with cream.

Season the potato soup again with salt and pepper. Cut the cooked carrots into fine slices and add them to the finished potato soup.

25. Potato dumplings

104 kcal

Ingredients for 4 servings:

> 600g ∴ *floury potatoes*
>
> ∴ *80g potato starch*
>
> ∴ *1 egg*
>
> ∴ 2 teaspoons of *butter*
>
> ∴ *nutmeg*
>
> ∴ *salt, pepper*

Wash the potatoes and cook for 20 minutes at 100 ° in the perforated steamer. Peel while hot and press through the potato press. Mix with cornstarch, salt, egg, butter, pepper and nutmeg. Shape the mixture into 8 dumplings of the same size, steam in the perforated cooking basket for 20 minutes at 100 °.

Potato dumplings go well with many meat dishes, perfect with roast pork, wild boar, duck or goose.

26. Semolina dumplings

497 kcal

Ingredients for 4 servings:

> ∴ *250g wheat semolina*
>
> ∴ *100g butter*
>
> ∴ *180ml milk*
>
> ∴ *3 eggs*

∴ nutmeg

∴ salt

Mix all ingredients in a bowl and let steep for 10-15 minutes. Shape approx. 12 semolina dumplings and carefully place in the perforated steamer. Steam for 15 minutes at 100 ° C.

27. Stuffed zucchini

379 kcal

Ingredients for 4 servings:

∴ *2 zucchini*

∴ *1 cup of rice*

∴ *250g sheep cheese*

∴ *2* tbsp *herbs*

∴ *8* tablespoons of pureed *tomatoes*

∴ *2* tbsp *olive oil*

∴ *salt, pepper*

Wash the zucchini, cut in half and scoop out with a small spoon. Place the pulp in a bowl and set aside. Cook rice according to the instructions on the packet. Crumble the sheep cheese, mix with the tomatoes and season with salt and pepper. Stir in the oil. Mix the zucchini pulp with the rice and tomato mixture. Fill the zucchini with the mixture, sprinkle with herbs. Cook on the cooking plate of the steamer for 30 minutes at 100 °.

28. Spicy leek casserole - a light vegetarian dish

254 kcal

Ingredients for 4 servings:
  ∴ *1 leek*
  ∴ *170g buckwheat*
  ∴ *300ml vegetable stock*
  ∴ *250g* low-fat quark
  ∴ *3 eggs*
  ∴ *garlic powder*
  ∴ *salt, pepper*

Wash the buckwheat and steam it in the closed cooking basket with hot vegetable stock for 10 minutes at 100 °. Mix the quark with the eggs. Wash and clean the leek and cut into rings. Mix the cooled buckwheat with the quark and leek. Season with salt, pepper and garlic powder. Cook for 25 minutes at 100 °.

29. Bread dumplings

436 kcal

Ingredients for 4 servings:
- ∴ *300g diced* breadcrumbs
- ∴ *500ml milk*
- ∴ *1/2 bunch of parsley*
- ∴ *1 onion*
- ∴ *2 eggs*
- ∴ *25g butter*
- ∴ *butter for the mold*
- ∴ *salt*

Pour warm milk over the bread cubes in a bowl and let them steep for about 30 minutes. Coat the steamer with butter. Peel and chop the onion and sauté in butter. Wash the parsley, shake dry and finely chop.

Add onions, eggs, salt and parsley to the bread cubes and knead. Shape the dough into dumplings with moistened hands. Cook in the perforated steamer for 20 minutes at 100 °.

30. Carinthian lentil soup

232 kcal

Ingredients for 4 servings:

∴ *200g lentils*
∴ *1 liter of water*
∴ *1 clove of garlic*
∴ *1 onion*
∴ *1 teaspoon savory*
∴ *1 teaspoon thyme*
∴ *1 teaspoon basil*
∴ *1 bay leaf*
∴ *2* tablespoons of larded *bacon*
∴ *1* teaspoon *salt*
∴ *vinegar*

Soak the lentils in water the day before. Cook the lentils with all the spices except the salt and vinegar with the water in the closed steamer for 45 minutes at 100 °. Peel onion and garlic and chop finely. Sweat both in hot lard. Dust with flour and stir well. Add the roux to the soup, season with salt and vinegar.

Desserts and sweets

From pudding to yeast dumplings to jam, everything can be prepared in the steamer in an energy-saving and vitamin-friendly way. Sweet treats belong on the Sunday table and are comforting for the soul and food for the nerves. Here you will find 15 delicious recipes for working and lazy people with a sweet tooth.

1. Plum dumplings

787 kcal

Ingredients for 4 servings:
1000g ∴ *floury potatoes*
∴ *220g grippy flour*
∴ *50g wheat semolina*
∴ *1 egg*
∴ *130g butter*
∴ *20 plums*
∴ *200g breadcrumbs*
∴ *salt*

For the potato dough, wash the potatoes and cook in the perforated steamer for 30 minutes at 100 ° until soft. Wash, dry, halve and core the plums.

Peel the boiled potatoes while they are still warm and press them through the potato press. Knead quickly to a dough with the flour, semolina, salt, butter and egg on a floured work surface.

Divide the dough into even pieces, first shape a ball, press flat, put a plum in the middle and form dumplings. Put the dumplings in a buttered, perforated cooking basket and cook for 25 minutes at 100 degrees.

Heat the butter in a pan and lightly brown the crumbs in it. Roll the finished dumplings in the breadcrumbs and sprinkle with sugar.

2. Warm chocolate cake with a liquid core

493 kcal

Ingredients for 4 servings:
- ∴ *150g chocolate*
- ∴ *60g butter*
- ∴ *40g flour*
- ∴ *3 eggs*
- ∴ *90g powdered sugar*
- ∴ *Strawberries for garnish*
- Icing ∴ *sugar for sprinkling*

Break the chocolate into pieces and melt in the closed steamer for 10 minutes at 70 °. Melt the butter and mix it with the chocolate. Separate eggs. Beat egg whites until stiff. Mix the egg yolk, sugar and flour and mix with the chocolate. Fold in the egg whites. Fill dough into molds and place in a closed cooking basket. Steam for 30 minutes at 90 °. Turn the molds out while they are still warm, let the cake cool down a bit and garnish with strawberries and powdered sugar.

3. Quark soufflé

111 kcal

Ingredients for 4 servings:
∴ *280g quark*
∴ *4 eggs*
zest of ∴ *half a lemon*
∴ *80g sugar*
∴ *1* teaspoon *butter*

Separate eggs. Mix the egg yolk, lemon zest and quark together well. Beat the egg whites with the sugar until stiff and fold into the quark mixture. Butter 8 soufflé molds and sprinkle with powdered sugar. Pour in the quark mass and cover with heat-resistant foil. Cook on the steamer's cooking plate for 20 minutes at 90 °.

4. Cottage cheese dumplings

501 kcal

Ingredients for 4 servings:
- ∴ *500g quark*
- ∴ *140g butter*
- ∴ *2 eggs*
- ∴ *150g breadcrumbs*
- ∴ *2* tbsp *powdered sugar*
- ∴ *salt*

In a bowl, knead the quark, butter, eggs, breadcrumbs, salt and sugar into a smooth dough. Let the dough rest for half an hour. Shape the dough into dumplings and cook in the perforated basket for 12 minutes at 95 °.

5. Chocolate soufflé with a caramel core

461 kcal

Ingredients for 4 servings:
- ∴ *1 bar of chocolate with caramel filling*
- ∴ *200g cooking chocolate*
- ∴ *60g butter*
- ∴ *200g brown sugar*
- ∴ *3 eggs*

∴ 5 tbsp *flour*

∴ *milk*

Melt the cooking chocolate in the closed steamer for 10 minutes at 65 °. Separate eggs, beat egg whites until stiff. Whip the egg yolks with butter and sugar until creamy. Mix the melted chocolate with the egg yolk cream very well. Fold in the flour and a dash of milk, the mixture should be creamy. Finally fold in the egg whites. Pour half of the mixture into soufflé molds, add a piece of caramel chocolate and fill up with the rest of the batter. Place the molds in the steamer and steam for 30 minutes at 100 °.

6. Rhubarb compote with lavender sugar

- impresses with its simple preparation and extravagant taste
124 kcal

Ingredients for 4 servings:

∴ *1000g rhubarb*

∴ 2 tbsp *lavender* sugar

∴ 2 tbsp granulated *sugar*

∴ 2 tbsp *vanilla sugar*

Cut the rhubarb unpeeled into oblique pieces approx. 1-2 cm

long and place in a heat-resistant plastic bag with the sugar. Let it steep in the refrigerator for at least 30 minutes. Place the closed bag in the steamer and cook for 30 minutes at 60 °. Enjoy garnished with a peppermint leaf.

7. Custard

601 kcal

Ingredients for 4 servings:
- ∴ *130g butter*
- ∴ *130g sugar*
- ∴ *2 egg yolks*
- ∴ 1 pk. *baking powder*
- ∴ 2 pk. *vanilla sugar*
- ∴ *120g flour*
- ∴ *250ml milk*
- ∴ *50g* cornstarch

Mix the butter with the sugar. Gradually mix in the egg yolks. Mix the flour with baking powder and stir in with the vanilla sugar and milk until a creamy mixture is formed.

Grease the rice container of the steamer and add the pudding mixture, cover with cling film.

Put the container in the steamer and steam for 80 minutes at 65 °. Serve garnished with fresh fruits and chocolate sauce.

8. Nut noodles

587 kcal

Ingredients for 4 servings:
- ∴ *750g potatoes*
- ∴ *3 eggs*
- ∴ *8* tbsp *wholemeal flour*
- ∴ *180g walnuts*
- ∴ *3* tbsp *powdered sugar*
- ∴ *salt*

Steam the potatoes with their skins in the perforated cooking basket for 25 minutes at 100 °. Peel while hot and press through the potato press. Add eggs and flour to the potatoes, season with salt and knead everything into a light dough. Shape the dough into a roll, cut off small slices and roll out pasta about 1cm thick. Steam the pasta in the perforated cooking basket for 20 minutes at 100 °. Grate walnuts and mix powdered sugar. Turn the cooked noodles in the nut mixture until they are completely covered.

Tip: You can also use poppy seeds instead of nuts, for a classic

9. Apricot dumplings - a specialty from the Wachau

826 kcal

Ingredients for 4 servings:
- ∴ *12 apricots*
- ∴ *500g quark*
- ∴ *2 eggs*
- ∴ *10* tbsp *flour*
- ∴ *300g breadcrumbs to sprinkle on*
- ∴ *10* tablespoons of *breadcrumbs for the dough*
- ∴ *200g butter*
- ∴ *salt*

Mix the quark, eggs, flour, 10 tablespoons of breadcrumbs and salt with the mixer. Let the dough rest in the refrigerator for 30 minutes. Wash and dry the apricots. Sprinkle the work surface with flour, roll out the dough and divide into 12 equal pieces. Shape each piece of dough into a circle, place an apricot in the middle and fold the dough around it to form a dumpling. Steam in the perforated steamer for 20 minutes at 100 °. Melt the butter slowly in a pan, it shouldn't turn brown! Add the breadcrumbs and brown them lightly. Roll the dumplings in the butter crumbs and serve sprinkled with sugar.

Tip: If the apricots are very sour, open the fruit halfway, remove the core and replace with a lump of sugar!

10. Exotic rice pudding

427 kcal

Ingredients for 4 servings:
- ∴ *250g rice* pudding
- ∴ *300ml coconut water*
- ∴ *350ml milk*
- ∴ 5 tbsp *maple syrup*
- ∴ *300g pineapple*
- ∴ *5 dates*
- ∴ 2 teaspoons of *coconut flakes*

Put the rice pudding in the closed container of the steamer. Mix the milk, coconut water and maple syrup and pour over the rice. Steam for 30 minutes at 100 °.

Meanwhile, peel the pineapple and cut into small pieces. Chop the dates and coconut flakes in a blender. Serve the finished rice pudding with pineapple and dates.

11. Almond wedges

207 kcal

Ingredients for 4 servings:
- ∴ *135g flour*
- ∴ *1 1/2* tbsp *brown sugar*
- ∴ *21 / 2g dry yeast*
- ∴ *1 egg*
- ∴ *25g almond butter*
- ∴ *70ml milk*
- ∴ *salt*

Mix the flour, sugar, salt and yeast together. Mix the milk, egg and almond butter in a bowl and knead everything together to form a smooth dough. Cover the dough with a clean cloth and let rise in a warm place for 30 minutes. Dust a work surface with flour, knead the dough well again and divide into 4 portions. Grease the perforated steam container. Shape each portion into a ball and place in the steamer. Cover and let rise for another 10 minutes, then steam for 20 minutes at 65 °.

12. Pumpkin and apple jam

60 kcal

Ingredients for 1000g of fruit:

∴ *700g pumpkin*

∴ *300g apples*

∴ *500g* preserving *sugar 2: 1*

∴ *lemon juice*

∴ *ginger*

∴ *nutmeg*

Peel and core the pumpkin and cut into small pieces. Cook in a closed container with a pinch of sugar at 100 ° for 12-15 minutes. Peel the apples, remove the core and cut into small pieces. Drizzle with lemon juice. After 15 minutes of cooking, add the apple pieces, preserving sugar, some grated ginger, nutmeg and lemon juice to the pumpkin pieces in the steamer and mix well. Steam for another 20 minutes at 100 °. Quickly puree the hot mass and pour into jam jars.

Tip: The recipe also works with other fruits such as apricots, strawberries or pears.

13. Yeast dumplings with Powidl

(Powidl = plum jam)
713 kcal

Ingredients for 4 servings:

∴ *30g yeast*

∴ 500g flour
∴ 60g sugar
∴ 60g butter
∴ 250ml milk
∴ 1 egg
∴ 1 egg yolk
∴ lemon peel
∴ 1 pk. vanilla sugar
∴ salt

For the fullness:
∴ 250g plum jam
∴ 150g poppy seeds
∴ rum
∴ 90g butter

Stir the yeast with a little flour and sugar into the lukewarm milk. Let rise in a warm place. Knead all remaining ingredients with the risen milk-yeast mixture. Shape the dough into a ball, sprinkle with flour and cover with a clean cloth. Let rise in a warm place for about 45 minutes.

For the filling, mix the plum jam with a good dash of rum. Divide the risen yeast dough into pieces of equal size and press flat with your hand. Place a tablespoon of the filling on each piece of dough and shape everything into a dumpling. Place the dumplings side by side in the greased, perforated steamer and cover and let rise for another 10 minutes. Then steam for 12 minutes at 100 °. Melt butter and brown lightly. Pour the melted butter over the finished dumplings and serve sprinkled with poppy seeds and sugar.

14. Steamed noodles - a southern German specialty.

732 kcal

Ingredients for 4 servings:
 ∴ *40g yeast*
 ∴ *500g flour*
 ∴ *250ml milk*
 80g ∴ *melted butter*
 ∴ *2 egg yolks*
 ∴ *sugar*
 ∴ *salt*
 ∴ *20g* melted *butter for brushing*

Put the flour in a bowl and make a well in the middle. Add yeast, milk and a little sugar and mix with a little flour. Cover with a cloth and let rise in a warm place for about 20 minutes. Then add the remaining ingredients and knead everything. Roll out the dough about 3 cm thick on a well-floured work surface. Cut out round steamed noodles with a drinking glass and brush with melted butter. Let rise for another

15 minutes. Steam the steamed noodles in the closed cooking basket for approx. 35 minutes at 95 ° degrees. Sprinkle with powdered sugar and serve with vanilla sauce.

15. Creme brulée

199 kcal

Ingredients for 4 servings:
  ∴ *8 egg yolks*
  ∴ *250ml cream*
  ∴ *200ml milk*
  ∴ 1 tbsp *brown cane sugar*
  ∴ *1 vanilla pod*
  ∴ 4 tbsp *brown sugar for sprinkling*

Heat the cream with the milk in a saucepan, but do not bring to the boil! Remove from heat and stir in egg yolks and sugar. Halve the vanilla pod lengthways and scrape out the pulp. Mix the vanilla pulp with the cream-milk mixture. Pour the liquid into small casserole dishes and steam in the closed steamer for 40 minutes at 90 °. Chill the cream for approx. 1 hour. Just before serving, sprinkle with brown sugar and caramelize with a kitchen bunsen burner.

Overview of cooking times:

Meat and poultry: 75 - 90 ° Celsius

∴ *Chicken breast fillet: 15 minutes*

∴ *Chicken* thighs: *40 minutes*

Turkey schnitzel ∴ : *35 minutes*

Roast ∴ *pork: 40 minutes*

Lamb ∴ *fillet: 14 minutes*

∴ *Knackwurst, Krainer: 6 minutes*

∴ *Frankfurter, Bockwurst: 10 minutes*

Fish and crustaceans: 75 - 90 ° Celsius

Fresh ∴ *fish fillets: 10 minutes*

Frozen ∴ *fish fillets: 18 minutes*

∴ *Tuna, fish steaks: 16 minutes*

∴ *Whole fish, fresh: 20 minutes*

∴ *Whole fish, TK: 26 minutes*

∴ *1 kg of fresh mussels: 20 minutes*

∴ *Shrimp, fresh: 5 minutes*

Shrimps ∴ *, frozen: 7 minutes*

Fresh ∴ *scallops: 5 minutes*

Rice and pasta: 100 ° Celsius with the addition of liquid (water, broth)

∴ *Long grain rice,* basmati *rice, rice* pudding: *20 minutes*

Risotto ∴ rice: 40 minutes
∴ Whole grain rice: 22 minutes
∴ Quick- cook rice, parboiled rice: 18 minutes
∴ Pasta: 20 minutes

Vegetables: 100 ° Celsius

∴ Artichokes, fresh: 43 minutes
∴ Eggplant, fresh: 10 minutes
∴ Cauliflower, fresh: 19 minutes
∴ Broccoli, fresh: 18 minutes
∴ Broccoli, frozen: 12 minutes
∴ Peas, fresh or frozen: 20 minutes
∴ Fennel: 22 minutes
Fresh ∴ beans: 30 minutes
Frozen ∴ beans: 25 minutes
∴ Potatoes, whole: 20 minutes
∴ Carrots, sliced or diced: 5 minutes
∴ Leeks: 30 minutes
∴ Corn on the cob, whole: 30 minutes
∴ Paprika: 15 minutes
∴ Mushrooms, fresh: 12 minutes
∴ Celery, fresh: 20 minutes
∴ Asparagus, fresh: 15 - 18 minutes
Fresh ∴ spinach: 10 minutes
Frozen ∴ spinach: 15 minutes
∴ Tomatoes: 6 minutes
∴ Zucchini: 12 minutes

Fruit: 100 ° Celsius

∴ Apples, fresh: 18 minutes

∴ Bananas, fresh: 12 minutes

∴ Pears, fresh: 20 minutes

∴ Rhubarb, fresh: 12 minutes

Other dishes: 65 - 100 ° Celsius

∴ Chocolate: 10 minutes

∴ Honey: 10 minutes

Hard-boiled ∴ egg: 12 minutes

∴ Egg, stone- soft: 6 minutes

Made in the USA
Monee, IL
26 July 2023